Birds of Yellowstone

BIRDS

OF

YELLOWSTONE

*A Practical Habitat Guide to
the Birds of Yellowstone National Park—
and where to find them*

by Terry McEneaney

Illustrations by Karen McEneaney

foreword by Dr. John Craighead

ROBERTS RINEHART, INC. PUBLISHERS

You have learnt from the birds and continue to learn;
Your best benefactors and early instructors.

Aristophanes

To The Memory of *Catherine McEneaney*

To my mother for her countless hours of driving me around in her car during my younger years of watching birds, and who instilled in me the belief that a unique harmony exists between people and birds.

Cover photo: Trumpeter Swans by Michael Quinton

author photo by Bill Doughty

Copyright© 1988 by Terry McEneaney
Published by Roberts Rinehart, Inc. Publishers
Post Office Box 3161   Boulder, Colorado 80303
ISBN 0-911797-44-0
Library of Congress Catalog Card Number 88-60322
Printed in the United States of America

Contents

Foreword

NATURE IS COMPLEX; ITS COMPONENTS, DIVERSE and interrelated. What we see in nature depends to a large extent on what we know. This book informs us that if we want to find birds we should know something about their habitats and how birds relate to them. Birds utilize specific habitat types. If you can recognize and find the habitats you can find and recognize the birds. A bird's habitat is its home, the biological and physical environment in which it lives. Through the evolutionary process bird species have adapted to their habitats; they are an integral part of them—like a glove to the hand. Therefore, the author advises us to look for habitats and then for birds. This method can be enjoyable and educational, and it widens our horizons. It can also save time in the field and make bird-finding easier.

Yellowstone supports four life zones with a great diversity of plant life. Some birds, like the Common Raven, the Great Horned Owl, and the American Robin, utilize a wide range of habitat types and can be found throughout the park, while others, like the Sage Thrasher and Harlequin Duck, have very specific habitat requirements and are, therefore, found in localized sites where their biological needs can be met. A most critical need is food and the habitat must supply it. Soon you learn to associate the food habits of a species with the habitat it prefers. For instance, to find the Clark's Nutcracker, you go to the high ridges of the Subalpine Zone to find whitebark pines that produce the pine nuts they prefer. To see the American Dipper you drop down the mountains to the small creeks and rivers of the Subalpine and Montane Zones. You then look for the shallow reaches and riffles that support the nymphs and larvae of aquatic insects. These are the dipper's food and the American Dipper is adapted in numerous ways to catch its food underwater in competition with trout and Rocky Mountain whitefish. The Peregrine Falcon is rare and you will be fortunate to see it. However, your chances are greatly increased if you find its habitat of cliffs overlooking water or large open meadows bordering streams and rivers. This falcon catches its prey in flight. The Peregrine is especially fond of shore birds and birds of open spaces. So, if you find the habitat of sandpipers, waterfowl, and swallows you have found the hunting habitats of the Peregrine Falcon and there you are most likely to see it.

Essentially, the author is telling us how to link birds with plants and plants with vegetation types in relation to topography, altitude, and seasons. In the process, we begin to see the myriad of interrelationships that Yellowstone's great diversity of life offers the keen observer. We transform ourselves from birders to ecologists, and, as such, we understand more of what we see. Moreover, we get a greater thrill from our efforts because we have not just added another bird to our species list but have followed ecological clues that have led us to our find. By developing an understanding of the complexity and the beauty of life, we learn to appreciate an unparalleled natural area preserved for all people for all time. If you use this book as the author intended, you cannot help but enjoy Yellowstone National Park and grow intellectually and aesthetically in the process.

The author has provided a bonus that should not be overlooked. He tells us the locations of the best roadside birding areas. This information is especially helpful to the novice birdwatcher, but it is also valuable to the experienced birder, to the expert, and to the professional ornithologist as well. Even the most adept birdwatcher can use tips and the author supplies these in abundance.

Dr. John Craighead
Craighead Wildlife—Wildlands Institute
Missoula, Montana

Preface

LET'S GO RUN THAT BIRD DOWN! SAID TEDDY Roosevelt, 26th president of the United States.

It was early April, 1903. The President had traveled to Yellowstone National Park to do some serious birding and wildlife-watching, perhaps to take his mind off the pressing affairs of state. His traveling companion was none other than John Burroughs, poet and naturalist of the lower Catskills, who, then at age 66, was enjoying a reputation as one of America's foremost nature writers. The two had heard a strange note or call "such as a boy might make by blowing in the neck of an empty bottle." The President led the scramble up the hillside to track down the mystery bird. There, calling from a tree, was a Pygmy Owl, the first the President had seen during his long career as a birder. He was ecstatic.

Since the creation of Yellowstone National Park in 1872, Yellowstone's wildlife and natural wonders have attracted the attention of the world's naturalists—besides Roosevelt and Burroughs, the roster includes C. Hart Merriam, Ernest Thompson Seton, John Muir, George Bird Grinnell, the Earl of Dunraven, Elliott Coues, and Adolph Murie, to name a few. Birders and wildlife enthusiasts from around the world have been drawn to Yellowstone, the world's first national park.

And small wonder. Yellowstone, with its diversity of habitats and its endlessly amazing natural features, is certainly one of the world's great wilderness/wildlife conservatories. When one considers the natural splendors Yellowstone has to offer—the mountains, the canyons, the rivers, the waterfalls, the lakes, the hot springs, and the geysers, coupled with a broad diversity of plant and animal life— superlatives are justified. There are certainly other places on earth where birds are more abundant and concentrated, or where a greater diversity of birds can be observed. But, where else can you watch an Osprey carrying a fish in its talons fly past a spectacular waterfall, or a Common Raven feeding on a bison carcass as a geyser erupts? Or where can you hear the simultaneous bugling of an elk, hooting of a Great Horned Owl, howling of a coyote, calling of a flock of Sandhill Cranes, and trumpeting of Trumpeter Swans in a dissonant but unforgettable wilderness concerto? Watching birds in Yellowstone is like going to a multi-media show.

The purpose of this book is to aid your enjoyment of Yellowstone's remarkably varied birdlife. In the introductory chapter, you will be given some helpful tips on bird-watching in general and on birding in Yellowstone in particular. Chapter 2 introduces you to the physiography, life-zones, vegetation, and habitats of the Park as they relate to bird distribution. Chapter 3 presents a gallery of portraits of twenty representative birds of the Park. Chapter 4 offers a roadside guide to birding in the Park. In chapter 5, the best birding areas of the park will be described in greater detail. Chapter 6 presents an easily-understood summary of ecological data on Yellowstone's birds. Incorporated into this data is a bird checklist, for those accustomed to seasonal abundance birding information. Near the end of this book is a sample "bird observation form" for those people who are interested in contributing new information on Yellowstone birds.

The order in which birds are listed and the names of the species conform with the latest classification of the American Ornithologists Union (6th edition 1983, 35th supplement 1985). These may differ from the sequence and names found in older field guides.

I sincerely hope that you, like Teddy Roosevelt, find moments of unforgettable discovery during your visit to Yellowstone. And I hope that this book adds measurably to your enjoyment of the Yellowstone experience.

Common Raven

Killdeer

1

ENJOYING
YELLOWSTONE'S BIRDLIFE

THIS BOOK IS FIRST AND FOREMOST A FINDER'S guide to Yellowstone birds. It has been designed to help you find birds during your stay in Yellowstone and to present you with detailed and accurate information on the birds you do find. The emphasis is on the habitat relations of Yellowstone's birds, since *an understanding of habitat is the key to successful bird-finding.* This book will also be your "tour guide," telling you what birds to expect as you travel through the Park. This book is **not** a field guide to identification; for help in field identification of Western birds please consult one of the following excellent field guides:

—*Birds of North America: A Guide to Field Identification*, by Chandler S. Robbins, B. Bruun, and H. S. Zim (New York: Golden Press, 1983).

—*Field Guide to the Birds of North America*, edited by Shirley L. Scott (Washington, D.C.: National Geographic Society, 1987).

—*A Field Guide to Western Birds*, by Roger T. Peterson (Boston: Houghton Mifflin, 1969).

—*The Audubon Society Master Guide to Birding*, edited by John Farrand Jr. (New York: Alfred Knopf, 1983), 3 volumes.

But this book has another important purpose as well. It is intended to provide a system for compiling new information gathered by the readers. It offers you the opportunity to contribute your detailed observations to a growing body of data on Yellowstone's birds. Over time, these bird obser-

Birding Areas of Yellowstone

vations will add significantly to our understanding of the distribution, abundance, movements, and ecology of the birds of Yellowstone National Park. This is therefore a *participatory* book, providing you the opportunity to participate in an ongoing, ever-growing study of Yellowstone's birds. In the back of the book you will find a sample bird observation form. Please consider using this format to share your discoveries of Yellowstone bird life with other interested birders. Your data will be carefully scrutinized and evaluated, and may be used in updating subsequent editions of this book.

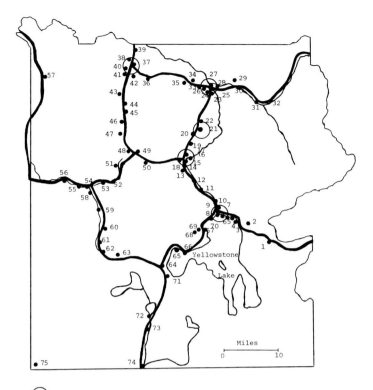

Location map of the best roadside birding areas in Yellowstone National Park.

Even though Yellowstone is a large area, it is still wild and relatively untouched by humans over the centuries. If we are to preserve natural treasures such as Yellowstone, we must work to ensure that our visit has the least possible impact. Please respect Yellowstone, its beautiful land-forms, and its sensational wildlife, so future generations can continue to enjoy it as one of the greatest wildlife won-derlands on earth.

In the following sections of this chapter, you will be given a brief overview on how to most effectively use this guide, and some tips will be offered to make your birding efforts more successful. Good luck and good birding.

HOW TO USE THIS GUIDE

To get the most out of your birding time in Yellowstone, take some time to become familiar with the general layout of this book before you set foot in the field. Read the complete text if you can, especially the section on habitat preferences. This will save you valuable time in the field. Study your field identification guide(s) so you will know the field marks of birds of particular interest to you. Look over chapter 3, which provides detailed profiles on some of the birds of interest that you are likely to encounter. Also, study the maps and lists of birding places in chapters 4 and 5: these sections might be useful to you in planning your route of travel through the Park. Last but not least, use the index.

To summarize, the following table will help you quickly find the information you need:

- TO FIND WHAT BIRDS TO EXPECT IN A PARTICULAR HABITAT – refer to chapter 2.
- TO FIND WHAT BIRDS TO LOOK FOR IN A PARTICULAR AREA – refer to chapter 4 and chapter 5.
- TO FIND SPECIFICS ON A PARTICULAR SPECIES – refer to chapter 6.
- TO FIND DETAILED INFORMATION ON THE TWENTY CHARACTERISTIC BIRDS OF YELLOWSTONE – refer to chapter 3.
- TO FIND THE BEST BIRDING SPOTS IN A PARTICULAR AREA OF THE PARK – refer to chapter 4, chapter 5, chapter 6, and look up the name of the area in the index.
- TO FIND SCIENTIFIC NAMES OF ALL BIRDS, MAMMALS, AND PLANTS DISCUSSED IN THIS BOOK – refer to field identification guides.
- TO FIND A GUIDED BIRDING TOUR ALONG THE ROADS OF YELLOWSTONE – refer to chapter 4.
- TO FIND WHAT BIRDS TO EXPECT DURING A PARTICULAR SEASON – refer to chapter 2 and chapter 6.
- TO FIND A BIRD CHECKLIST, BIRD ABUNDANCE, AND ECOLOGICAL INFORMATION CHARTS – refer to chapter 6.
- TO CONTRIBUTE YOUR FINDINGS TO A GROW-

ING SCIENTIFIC DATA BASE – use the observation form at the end of the book.

TIPS FOR THE BEGINNING BIRDWATCHER

Try not to let all these different species of birds overwhelm you. For best results learn to identify the more easily observed birds (i.e. Canada Goose, Mallard, American Robin, Killdeer, Red-winged Blackbird, etc.) and especially note the specific habitat(s) in which these birds are often found. Since all ducks are associated with water habitats, a highly recommended practice for the beginner is to learn the different species of ducks found in a particular area. Once one has mastered a particular group of birds in a particular habitat, try expanding into other groups of birds and other habitats.

SOME GENERAL BIRDING TIPS

When to Come. For the greatest diversity of birds: early June to early July, mid-August to mid-September. For observing autumn bird migration: mid-August to early November. For rare, unusual, or difficult to find birds: early May to mid-June, mid-August to early November.

What to Wear. Since Yellowstone makes its own weather, it is advisable to dress for the unexpected. Do not come to Yellowstone without cold-weather and wet-weather clothing. Remember, this is a high altitude plateau; a hat, warm gloves, heavy coat, and boots are a must.

Suggested Birding Items. A good pair of binoculars is essential. If you do not have binoculars you will miss many opportunities to view wildlife in Yellowstone. Purchasing binoculars is a wise investment; it opens up a whole new world for the observer. Birders in the past have often used 7×50 binoculars. Recently, however, birders have found 8- or 9- power binoculars provide more details and therefore greatly aid in the identification of birds. Other important items include; a bird identification guide, pencil or pen, and a notebook. Optional but useful birding items include a spotting scope and a camera.

Where to Stay. There are numerous campgrounds located within or adjacent to Yellowstone National Park. During the peak visitor use period (June through August), campsites in campgrounds can be difficult to find and are available on a first come-first serve basis. For best results and to avoid frustration, secure a campsite by noon of the night you intend to camp.

A number of excellent hotels and lodges are located within the boundaries of the Park. There is also a large selection of motels, lodges, and cabins located outside the Park in virtually every direction. During peak periods, however, reservations are strongly recommended.

Food and Fuel. Food and fuel can be found both within the Park and on its outskirts.

For more detailed information on all of these services, consult a Park brochure, which can be obtained at any entrance to Yellowstone National Park or by writing: Superintendent, Yellowstone National Park, Wyoming 82190. For information concerning areas adjacent to Yellowstone National Park, consult a local chamber of commerce.

Narrowing the Possibilities. Learn to identify birds by the process of elimination. The following mnemonic phrase will assist you in narrowing down the possibilities by asking five important questions. Bird identification will come easy for you if you remember this slogan, ***Habitat Birding Is The Answer.***

H = What *habitat* is the bird utilizing? What birds would use this type of *habitat*?

B = What *group of birds* or *family ancestral branch of birds* does this bird belong to?

I = What are the key *individual identification characteristics* of this bird?

T = Is the bird normally found here this *time of year*?

A = Is this bird normally found in this geographic *area*?

Time of Day. The time to watch birds depends on the time of year and the species you are trying to find. For general purposes, in the summer the greatest diversity of birds can be found during the first three hours after sunrise and the last two hours before sunset. The same rule is also effective for finding other wildlife in Yellowstone. This also happens to be the time of day with the least amount of vehicle traffic. During the autumn and winter, birding at midday is usually best.

Use Your Car as a Blind. Birds seen from the roads are normally accustomed to vehicles. A parked car serves as an excellent blind, and in many instances birds can be viewed more closely this way than they can be on foot. When watching birds from a car, remember to park in a safe place well away from the main flow of traffic. Always pull *completely* off the road.

Keep Quiet While Birding. For best bird watching results, remain as quiet as possible. Avoid loud conversations and be careful not to slam vehicle doors – this frightens birds away. If birding on foot, walk slowly and quietly. For best results, avoid wearing brightly-colored clothing if at all possible. Always be on the lookout for *bears* in Yellowstone. Bears are unpredictable and dangerous, so avoid bear conflicts whenever possible.

Birding Etiquette. A book on Yellowstone birds would not be complete without discussing the importance of watching birds without disturbing them. Anyone can watch birds, but the true birder has the ability and experience to observe birds without disrupting them. The following are some helpful tips on birding etiquette:

—The welfare of the bird is the most important consideration
—Use either binoculars or a spotting scope for observing birds; this lessens the chance of disturbance.
—Keep your distance. If the behavior of the bird changes due to your presence or if the bird flushes, then you are too close.
—*Do Not* disturb birds on or near nests.
—Avoid touching bird nests, eggs, or nestlings – human scent attracts mammalian predators.
—Avoid splitting up family groups of birds. This increases the chances of mortality.

Learn to "Read the Landscape." You do not have to travel long distances to find a great variety of birds. Learn to recognize bird habitats or changes in vegetation. Soon you will realize that the areas with the greatest diversity of vegetation usually have the greatest diversity of birdlife. For example, in Yellowstone the greatest diversity of vegetation is in the area of Mammoth, and there you will find the greatest variety of birds.

Attend Interpretive Programs. During the summer months, Yellowstone National Park offers interpretive programs on birdlife. For more details, inquire at the following visitor centers: Mammoth, Fishing Bridge, Old Faithful, and Canyon.

Photographing Birds. Professional photographers (but not amateurs) must obtain a permit for photographing wildlife in Yellowstone. By definition a professional photographer is one who makes money from selling photographs. For further information on obtaining a professional photographer's permit, contact: YNP Headquarters, Yellowstone National Park, Wyoming 82190.

WEATHER AND BIRDWATCHING

Knowing the weather and preparing for the elements is an important consideration for any traveler, especially a birdwatcher. *Yellowstone creates its own weather.* If you remember this basic rule you can't go wrong. In midsummer a perfectly clear hot day with blue skies can be suddenly transformed into a raging thunderstorm. In the winter, clear blue skies may quickly turn into a blizzard. Snowstorms in Yellowstone are not necessarily restricted to winter; as a matter of fact, snowstorms have been recorded in Yellowstone in every month of the year. Naturally the chances of a snowstorm are low in summer, but nevertheless one should come prepared – particularly if visiting Yellowstone early or late in the summer. Be prepared at all times for sudden changes in the weather. Such changes are the norm in such a high mountainous plateau.

Bird behavior is also influenced by weather patterns. A calm, sunny day is what every visitor dreams of, but it doesn't always happen. On a day with strong winds most birds have taken cover and are usually difficult to find. During such periods water birds have no place to hide except near the windward shore of a lake, or on the leeward side of natural barriers such as banks, beaches, vegetation. Birds are relatively inactive during severe rain and snowstorms. A calm after a storm is an excellent time to observe birds, particularly during the months when birds are migrating through Yellowstone. During the hottest days of summer, birds are most active in the early morning and late evening. On cold, overcast days bird activity is relatively slow, and efforts to observe them should be geared more to the mid-morning through mid-afternoon hours.

Mallard (drake) tail feather

2
YELLOWSTONE'S ENVIRONMENTS

ONE OF THE BIG ATTRACTIONS OF YELLOWstone National Park is the opportunity it offers to experience change – change from the familiar surroundings near home to something completely different. Yellowstone offers three exciting elements of change: change in climate, in topography, and in vegetation. This concept of "change" was first developed in 1924 by Grinnell and Storer. As you travel from one area of Yellowstone to another, you will notice gradual but dramatic changes in these elements. In traveling from the lower elevation near Gardiner to the summit of Mt. Washburn, for example, you will encounter everything from arid grasslands, to open and forested areas, to low growing alpine vegetation. Associated with these environmental changes are distinct changes in the wildlife species. This chapter introduces you to the variety of habitats that is to be found in Yellowstone and describes the types of birds you can expect in different habitats. An understanding of the relationships of birds to their physical environment is the key to successful birding and the focus of this book.

In order to understand the distribution of Yellowstone's birds it is important to understand and be familiar with their habitat requirements. Little is known about the reasons birds select certain habitats over others, but we do know that a bird's jizz, physical structure, and evolutionary history are all related to its environment, and the environment where its ancestors once lived. As you travel through Yellowstone think of birds in terms of their habitats, and especially of their food requirements. For example, Common Loons are fish-eaters and are usually found on large lakes that contain fish, while Western Meadowlarks feed on insects and are found primarily in grasslands. Your chances of finding a particular bird increase greatly if you know its habitat requirements, and your knowledge of habitat relationships can save you much time in the identification of a particular bird species.

Read the material in this chapter *before* you set out after birds; I guarantee you will find more species and enjoy the experience more thoroughly. This chapter relates Yellowstone bird distribution to topography, climate, and vegetation, and provides you with a series of "habitat profiles" describing birds found in typical habitats.

GEOLOGY AND TOPOGRAPHY

The origin of Yellowstone's birds is closely tied to the origin of the Yellowstone landscape. The vegetation and wildlife that are commonly found in Yellowstone today are the result of long evolutionary processes of adaptation to a changing mountain environment. Keefer (1984) described the geologic processes that took place in Yellowstone. Approximately 600,000 years ago a violent volcanic eruption shook this mountainous area. The sudden explosion forced tremendous quantities of hot volcanic ash and pumice to the earth's surface, devastating the landscape and vegetation. This catastrophic eruption left two large magma chambers that were vented on the earth's surface. The roofs of these magma chambers collapsed, forming a large smoldering crater called a caldera, which measured thirty miles across and forty-five miles wide.

The earth's magma worked its way through the ring fracture zones surrounding the caldera. Numerous fractures in these zones allowed the lava to ooze out onto the surface and fill in the caldera, forming what is known as the Yellowstone Plateau. Today these fracture zones provide an important system of underground channels for the circulation of hot water throughout Yellowstone. Hot springs, geysers, and other thermal features are a reminder of the link between past and present volcanic activity.

Following the mountain building and volcanic episodes, there occurred periods of extreme glaciation, which eroded the landscape and changed the face of Yellowstone. Geologists have theorized that Yellowstone was glaciated at least three times in the last 300,000 years. The most recent, the Pinedale glaciation, occurred approximately 25,000 years ago and covered most of what is today Yellowstone National Park. An icecap estimated to be 3,000 feet thick was centered over the Yellowstone Lake area. As the temperature warmed and the ice melted, the icecap and glaciers began shrinking. The glaciers gradually retreated up the mountain valleys until 8,500 years ago, when they totally disappeared. Today no glaciers exist in the Park, but evidence of past glaciation and melting is apparent throughout the extreme northern section of the Yellowstone landscape.

According to Despain (1973), the two major types of bedrock that occur in Yellowstone today are the Absaroka and Yellowstone volcanics. Spruce-fir forests are associated with Absaroka andesitic rocks and soils, which are high in minerals and stimulate plant growth. Lodgepole pine forests are associated with the Yellowstone rhyolitic rocks and soils, which are low in minerals and consequently minimize plant growth.

CLIMATE

The sun is the ultimate source of the earth's energy and is perhaps the greatest single influence on the earth's climate. In Yellowstone the climate is undoubtedly controlled by the sun, but it is also influenced by air masses. Yellowstone lies between 44 degrees and 45 degrees north latitude, which is approximately halfway between the equator and the north pole. During the longer days of summer, the Yellowstone landscape absorbs the greatest amount of solar heat and the dominant air masses come from the south. In the winter, with its shorter days, the Yellowstone landscape absorbs the least amount of solar heat and the air masses come from more northerly latitudes.

Since Yellowstone is a high elevation mountain plateau, altitude plays an important role in solar heat retention and radiation. There is a general rule that for every thousand feet of elevational gain there is a net loss of 3 1/2 degrees F. in temperature. Therefore at higher elevations there is a greater loss of solar radiation, and an even greater loss in solar radiation from daytime to nighttime and from summer to winter. It is these high altitudinal conditions at mid-latitude that give Yellowstone its justifiable reputation of having a harsh climate.

Loren Eiseley once wrote "If there is magic on this planet, it is contained in water." Precipitation, mostly in the form of snow, is the driving force of Yellowstone and an essential ingredient for all life forms. Precipitation is very closely related to elevation in this high mountain environment. The region of highest precipitation is the south portion of the Park. Other regions receive less precipitation because of the numerous mountain ranges that lie in their path as the storms work their way predominantly from west to east. In the south, once the storms travel easterly across the Snake River plains, they deposit large amounts of precipitation on the high plateaus of southern Yellowstone, since there are no major mountain ranges lying in the way.

LIFE ZONES AND VEGETATION

Yellowstone is a high mountain ecosystem, and as with all mountain ecosystems of any great relief, sweeping changes in the environment occur as one moves vertically up or down the mountain slopes. These changes lead to the concept of climatic or altitudinal zones.

For over a century, naturalists working in the Rocky Mountains have noted that the changes in vegetation one encounters in traveling up a mountainside are not random but seem to follow a pattern. Different attempts have been made to describe this phenomenon with some degree of precision. The "life zone" concept developed by C. Hart Merriam, one of the first biologists to explore Yellowstone in the late 19th century, best describes the relation of Yellowstone's plant and animal communities to topography, climate, and elevation. It provides an excellent framework for understanding the distribution of birds and bird habitats in Yellowstone National Park.

Life zones on a mountain can in many instances be compared to zones of latitude on the surface of the earth. For example, Mount Kilimanjaro (19,336 feet), located along the equator in Africa, includes all the life zones that would be encountered on a trip from the equator to the Arctic Circle. The further north one travels from the equator, the lower the altitude of the boundaries between the life zones. For example, timberline (the boundary between the sub-alpine and alpine zones) is at 10,000 feet in Yellowstone National Park and at 7,600 feet in Glacier National Park 260 miles to the north.

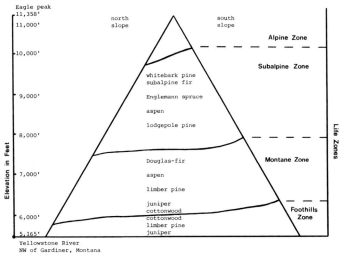

Fig. 1. Forested habitats in Yellowstone.

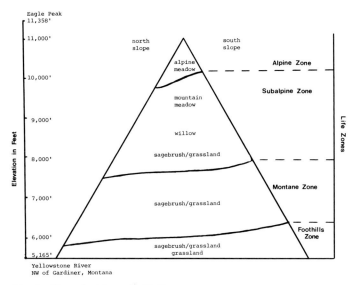

Fig. 2. Open habitats in Yellowstone.

YELLOWSTONE'S ENVIRONMENTS

Four life zones are represented in Yellowstone National Park: the *foothills zone,* 5,165 to 6,000 feet; the *montane Zone* 6,000 to 7,600 feet; the *subalpine zone,* from 7,600 feet to timberline (approximately 10,000 feet); and the *alpine zone,* above timberline up the top of the highest peak (Eagle Peak, 11,358 feet). Each of these life zones supports a distinct association of plants and animals. Some plants and animals have a much wider range than others and occur in several zones, while a few species are largely restricted to one zone. By noting the distribution of certain plant species one can determine with some degree of certainty the elevation of an area as well as the birds associated with that particular life zone. Plant distribution determines to a large extent the distribution of birds in Yellowstone. In some cases plant communities merge into each other at their boundaries. It is at these ecotones (edges) that the greatest diversity of plant life and bird life occurs.

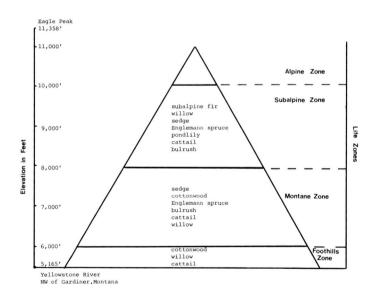

Fig. 3. Water/riparian habitats in Yellowstone.

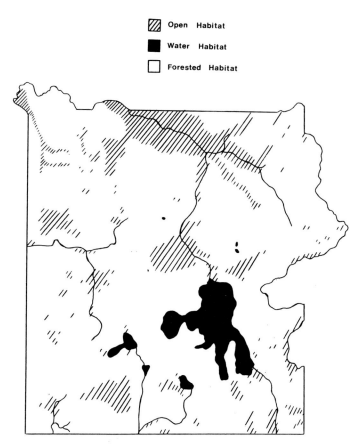

Open Habitat

Water Habitat

Forested Habitat

Fig. 4. Major open, water, and forested habitats of Yellowstone National Park.

The elevation of the boundaries between life zones is strongly influenced by the aspect, or the compass direction, a mountainside faces. At the latitude of Yellowstone National Park, north-facing slopes in general receive less radiation from the sun than do south-facing slopes and are therefore usually cooler and wetter. For this reason, a life zone boundary can be up to 700 feet higher on a south-facing slope than on a north-facing slope. This is shown in figures 1 and 2 which show the approximate elevations of the life zone boundaries on north- and south-facing slopes in Yellowstone Park. Figures 1 and 4 show which forested habitats to expect in the different life zones and the distri-

YELLOWSTONE'S ENVIRONMENTS

bution of these habitats. Figures 2 and 4 and figures 3 and 4 respectively show what kinds of open and water habitats to expect and where they are distributed in the Park. Refer to the vegetation identification charts (figures 5 and 6) for help in identifying major plant species. As shown in the map (figure 7), well over 90 percent of Yellowstone lies in the subalpine zone. Only a tiny area, near Gardiner/Mammoth, lies within the foothills zone. The life-zone concept is a very useful one in understanding Yellowstone bird distribution; the four life zones found in Yellowstone are discussed in more detail below.

The foothills zone (5,165-6,000 feet), also known as the "transition zone", is predominately open grassland and is found only in the vicinity of Mammoth and Gardiner. Scattered sagebrush and juniper are found at the upper to mid-levels of this zone. Also found sparingly in this zone, especially near Mammoth and along the Gardner River, are balsam poplar and narrowleaf cottonwood. At the upper reaches of the foothills zone, only sixteen to eighteen inches of precipitation fall annually. Near Gardiner, Montana, on the lower reaches of the foothills zone, Great Basin or "Cold Desert" vegetation is found. Greasewood, rabbitbrush, needle and thread and junegrass are commonly found in this relatively dry area where less than fifteen inches of precipitation are received annually. Soils are derived from shales and are subject to increased surface runoff.

The montane zone (6,000 to 7,600 feet), sometimes called the "Canadian zone," contains a combination of open and forested habitats. Douglas-fir is the dominant forest tree in this zone. The forest in this zone is characterized by mature, scattered, fire-scarred trees with an understory of snowberry, pine grass, and various wildflowers. Aspen are found in this zone. Englemann spruce and subalpine fir can be found along streams and creeks, as can occasional stands of lodgepole pine. Precipitation generally is between sixteen and twenty inches annually. Lightning-caused fires are common. Open areas, usually dominated by sagebrush, are more prevalent than forested areas. The soils in this zone are primarily glacial till, derived from the granites and volcanics found farther upstream.

FIGURE 5   IDENTIFICATION CHART OF THE MAJOR TREES OF YELLOWSTONE

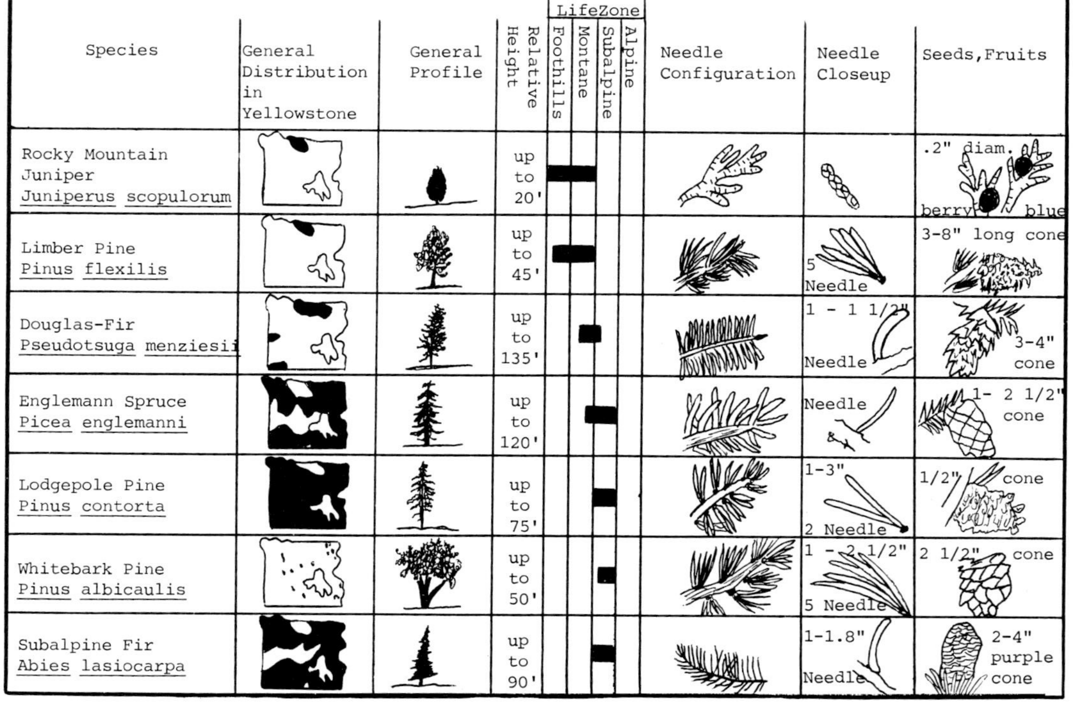

Species	General Distribution in Yellowstone	General Profile	Relative Height	Foothills	Montane	Subalpine	Alpine	Needle Configuration	Needle Closeup	Seeds, Fruits
Rocky Mountain Juniper Juniperus scopulorum			up to 20'	■	■					.2" diam. berry, blue
Limber Pine Pinus flexilis			up to 45'	■	■				5 Needle	3-8" long cone
Douglas-Fir Pseudotsuga menziesii			up to 135'		■				1 - 1 1/2" Needle	3-4" cone
Englemann Spruce Picea englemanni			up to 120'			■			1-3" Needle	1- 2 1/2" cone
Lodgepole Pine Pinus contorta			up to 75'		■				2 Needle	1/2" cone
Whitebark Pine Pinus albicaulis			up to 50'			■			1 - 2 1/2" 5 Needle	2 1/2" cone
Subalpine Fir Abies lasiocarpa			up to 90'			■			1-1.8" Needle	2-4" purple cone

Species	General Distribution in Yellowstone	General Profile	Relative Height	Life Zone				Leaf Configuration	Leaf Closeup	Buds, Flowers
				Alpine	Subalpine	Montane	Foothills			
Narrowleaf Cottonwood Populus angustifolia			up to 80'			■			2-3" long leaf / .5-1" wide	buds
Aspen Populus tremuloides			up to 60'		■				1-3" diam. leaf	buds
Willow Salix spp.			up to 20'			■			1-4" long leaf	flower
Big Sagebrush Artemesia tridentata			2-5' up to 10'		■				1 - 1 1/2" long leaf	flower

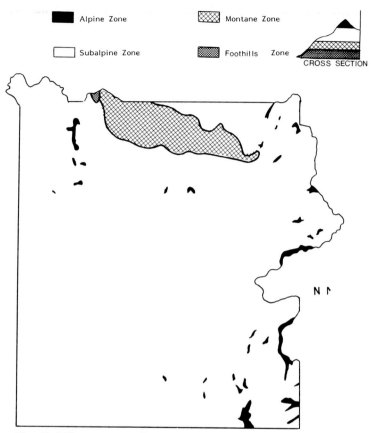

Legend:
- ■ Alpine Zone
- ▨ Montane Zone
- ☐ Subalpine Zone
- ▦ Foothills Zone

CROSS SECTION

N ▶

Fig. 7. Life zones or climatic zones of Yellowstone National Park.

The subalpine zone (7,600 to 10,000 feet), sometimes called the "Hudsonian zone," is mainly forested, interspersed with open areas. The subalpine zone can be further divided into two sub-zones based on precipitation, soils, elevation, and dominant forest tree species.

The *lodgepole pine* subzone (7,600 to 8,400) is dominated primarily by lodgepole pine, by far the most abundant tree in Yellowstone. Very little spruce or fir occur in the understory. Soils in this region are underlain by rhyolite, which is a well-drained, nutritionally poor soil. The nature of the soils, coupled with low annual precipitation (twenty to forty inches annually), account for the slow-growing nature of lodgepole pines in Yellowstone. Vegeta-

20   YELLOWSTONE'S ENVIRONMENTS

Fig. 7A. Sagebrush-grassland of the foothills zone. Author photo.

Fig. 7B. Sagebrush-grassland of the montane zone. Author photo.

tion on the forest floor consists of grouse whortleberry, elk sedge, and pine grass. Whitebark pine may also be present to some degree in both the overstory and understory. In areas where moisture accumulates (drainages, north-facing slopes, water edges), spruce-fir stands can some-times be found. Fire records indicate that most fires start and burn in spruce-fir stands in the montane and subalpine zones.

Fig. 7C. Lodgepole pine, subalpine zone. Author photo.

The *spruce-fir* subzone (8,400 feet to timberline) is dominated by various successional stages of Englemann spruce and subalpine fir. Lodgepole pine is also present in various degrees, but it is not as obvious because it is represented almost entirely by very young trees in the understory. Whitebark pine becomes a major component of this forest type, especially near timberline. Soils in this area are derived from andesitic bedrock, and rainfall exceeds forty inches annually. Because of these moist, fertile soils, the vegetation on the forest floor is much more diverse. Plants commonly found in the understory include grouse whortleberry, globe huckleberry, and a variety of wildflowers.

The alpine zone (10,000 to 11,358), sometimes referred to as the "Arctic zone," is that treeless area found above timberline. Vegetation in this zone is low to the ground and growth is often stunted. Plants are predominantly grasses and sedges interspersed with a small variety of wildflowers. This zone is dominated by tundra, meltwater meadows, and rock or fellfields. As one ascends to the upper limits of this zone, the climate becomes steadily more severe, culminating in arctic-like conditions found on the highest peaks in Yellowstone. At this level, snowbanks, freezing temperatures, and strong winds can be found almost every month of the year (Figure 8).

YELLOWSTONE'S ENVIRONMENTS

Fig. 7D. Subalpine fir, subalpine zone. Author photo.

Anomalies or exceptions in life-zone boundaries.
Zones of vegetation are influenced by local conditions such as temperature, precipitation, prevailing winds, exposure, bedrock, soils, and topography. Temperature has probably more influence than any other single physical factor. Timberline can be found much higher on a south-facing slope of a timbered creek than on a north-facing windswept ridge. As discussed earlier, vegetation is highly influenced by the type of bedrock present. Numerous natural geologic processes have created vegetative abnormalities or discontinuities in the vegetative zones. Glacial activity, particularly in the northern section of the park, has covered bedrock with glacial till and has caused vegetative types to overlap. Water areas created by glaciated terrain have created unusual departures from classic zones of vegetation. This is evident particularly in the Lamar Valley and along the lower reaches of the Yellowstone River.

Pelican and Hayden Valleys, two large open meadows located within the subalpine zone, are fine examples of departures from the expected zones of vegetation. These two sagebrush-grassland areas are underlain by thick deposits of lake sediments and are actually ancient lake beds from the ice age. Two other examples show the extension of a life zone below its expected elevational limit. One is an area near the West Entrance, where lodgepole pine of the subalpine zone extends down as low as 6,600 feet. The reason for this abnormality is the rhyolitic nature of the soils and the large amount of precipitation and cold air that accumulates in this area. Another is in the Bechler region of Yellowstone, where spruce-fir of the subalpine zone extends to as low as 6,100 feet. This is also due to the nature of the soils and the high amount of precipitation associated with the southern section of Yellowstone.

VEGETATION AND THE DISTRIBUTION OF BIRDS

Yellowstone is a complex mosaic of habitats. The delineation of these major habitats determines the geographic distribution of plants and associated wildlife. Local variations in climate and topographic features (such as creeks, lakes, rivers, waterfalls, cliffs, canyons, geyser basins, etc.) result in breaks or discontinuities in the climax vegetation so that small isolated plant communities become established. Discontinuities in the major vegetative types are very important influences on bird distribution. Natural forces such as lightning-caused fires, insect infestations, tree diseases, avalanches, windfalls, earthquakes, and thermal eruptions are often responsible for creating openings in the extensive forest canopy. In Yellowstone, fire has been largely responsible for the unique diversity in vegetative types.

Very rarely is there an abrupt change in the vegetation at the boundary where two distinct types of vegetation meet. More often they overlap. The edges, or ecotones, thus created are typically areas where the greatest variety of plant life occurs. They offer more food and cover per square foot than do the more uniform, or monotypic, stands of vegetation. It is also in these areas that the greatest variety of birdlife can be found. This attraction of numerous wildlife species to the ecotones is commonly referred to as the "edge effect."

Some Yellowstone birds have narrow habitat requirements and are able to adapt only to specific environmental conditions (examples: Sage Thrasher, Harlequin Duck). Other birds have the ability to occupy a diversity of habitat types (Examples: House Wren, American Robin, Common Raven, Chipping Sparrow). Different birds have evolved

Fig. 7E. The summit of Mt. Washburn showing timberline and the alpine zone. Author photo.

Fig. 8. A view of Electric Peak (10,992') from the northeast, and the delineation of the four climatic zones (foothills, montane, subalpine, and alpine) that are characteristically found in Yellowstone National Park. Author photo.

over time to occupy different niches within the same type of habitat. Odum (1959) explained these terms by simply stating that a bird's habitat is its address, and its niche is what it does for a living.

In the following pages, specific vegetation types and other "mini habitats" within the four major life zones are described. The types of *birds you are likely to encounter in the summer* are presented according to habitat types.

Habitats Of The Foothills Zone

Birds Associated with Grasslands

Red-tailed Hawk	Cliff Swallow
Golden Eagle	Common Raven
Prairie Falcon	Rock Wren
Horned Lark	Western Meadowlark

Birds Associated with Sagebrush-Grasslands (areas of sagebrush, sagebrush-grassland, or sagebrush-greasewood-saltbrush)

Red-tailed Hawk	Sage Thrasher
Golden Eagle	Western Meadowlark
Prairie Falcon	Brewer's Blackbird
Common Nighthawk	Horned Lark
Black-billed Magpie	Cliff Swallow
Common Raven	Vesper Sparrow
Rock Wren	Brewer's Sparrow

Birds Associated with Riparian Habitats (thickets along streamsides and river banks consisting of cottonwoods, willow, wild rose, etc.)

American Kestrel	American Dipper
Mallard	Mountain Bluebird
Killdeer	American Robin
Spotted Sandpiper	European Starling
Great Horned Owl	Warbling Vireo
Belted Kingfisher	Yellow Warbler
Downy Woodpecker	Yellow-rumped Warbler
Northern Flicker	Common Yellowthroat
Tree Swallow	MacGillivray's Warbler
Cliff Swallow	Lazuli Bunting
Northern Rough-winged Swallow	Chipping Sparrow

Black-billed Magpie
Common Raven
Black-capped Chickadee
House Wren

Song Sparrow
Brewer's Blackbird
Brown-headed Cowbird

Habitats Of The Montane Zone

Birds Associated with Sagebrush-Grasslands

Red-tailed Hawk
Golden Eagle
Prairie Falcon
Common Nighthawk
Horned Lark
Cliff Swallow
Black-billed Magpie
Common Raven

Rock Wren
Sage Thrasher
European Starling
Vesper Sparrow
Brewer's Sparrow
Western Meadowlark
Brewer's Blackbird
Brown-headed Cowbird

Birds Associated with Juniper (areas consisting of juniper or juniper-sagebrush)

Red-tailed Hawk
Golden Eagle
Prairie Falcon
Black-billed Magpie

Green-tailed Towhee
Chipping Sparrow
Dark-eyed Junco

Birds Associated with Limber Pine-Juniper

Red-tailed Hawk
Golden Eagle
American Kestrel
Great Horned Owl
Common Nighthawk
Red-naped Sapsucker
Williamson's Sapsucker
Hairy Woodpecker
Three-toed Woodpecker
Northern Flicker
Tree Swallow
Clark's Nutcracker
Black-billed Magpie

Common Raven
Mountain Chickadee
Red-breasted Nuthatch
White-breasted Nuthatch
Ruby-crowned Kinglet
Mountain Bluebird
Townsend's Solitaire
American Robin
Yellow-rumped Warbler
Chipping Sparrow
Dark-eyed Junco
Cassin's Finch
Pine Siskin

Birds Associated with Riparian Habitats (thickets along streamsides and river banks, consisting of Englemann spruce, cottonwood, or willow)

American Kestrel	House Wren
Mallard	Mountain Bluebird
Killdeer	American Robin
Spotted Sandpiper	American Dipper
Great Horned Owl	European Starling
Common Nighthawk	Warbling Vireo
Belted Kingfisher	Yellow Warbler
Red-naped Sapsucker	Yellow-rumped Warbler
Downy Woodpecker	MacGillivray's Warbler
Hairy Woodpecker	Common Yellowthroat
Northern Flicker	Lazuli Bunting
Tree Swallow	Chipping Sparrow
Northern Rough-winged Swallow	Lincoln's Sparrow
Cliff Swallow	Red-winged Blackbird
Black-billed Magpie	Cassin's Finch
Common Raven	Pine Siskin

Birds Associated with Aspen, Aspen-Willow

Cooper's Hawk	European Starling
Swainson's Hawk	Warbling Vireo
Ruffed Grouse	Yellow Warbler
Sandhill Crane	Yellow-rumped Warbler
Red-naped Sapsucker	MacGillivray's Warbler
Hairy Woodpecker	Common Yellowthroat
Western Wood Peewee	Chipping Sparrow
Willow Flycatcher	Lincoln's Sparrow
Dusky Flycatcher	White-crowned Sparrow
Tree Swallow	Dark-eyed Junco
Mountain Chickadee	Pine Siskin
House Wren	
Mountain Bluebird	

Birds Associated with Douglas-Fir

Northern Goshawk	Red-breasted Nuthatch
Cooper's Hawk	Ruby-crowned Kinglet
Red-tailed Hawk	Mountain Bluebird
Blue Grouse	American Robin
Great Horned Owl	Townsend's Solitaire
Great Gray Owl	Swainson's Thrush

Northern Saw-whet Owl
Williamson's Sapsucker
Hairy Woodpecker
Northern Flicker
Olive-sided Flycatcher
Hammond's Flycatcher
Clark's Nutcracker
Common Raven

Yellow-rumped Warbler
Western Tanager
Chipping Sparrow
Dark-eyed Junco
Cassin's Finch
Red Crossbill
Pine Siskin
Evening Grosbeak

Birds Associated with a Montane Pond (open areas of water surrounded by emergent vegetation such as sedges, rushes, or cattails)

Northern Harrier
Pied-billed Grebe
Trumpeter Swan
Canada Goose
Green-winged Teal
Mallard
Blue-winged Teal
Cinnamon Teal
Gadwall
American Wigeon
Ring-necked Duck
Lesser Scaup
Barrow's Goldeneye
Ruddy Duck

Sora
American Coot
Sandhill Crane
Killdeer
American Avocet
Common Snipe
Wilson's Phalarope
Common Nighthawk
Cliff Swallow
Common Raven
Red-winged Blackbird
Yellow-headed Blackbird
Brewer's Blackbird

Habitats Of The Subalpine Zone

Birds Associated with Sagebrush-Grassland

Swainson's Hawk
Red-tailed Hawk
Cliff Swallow
Common Raven

Vesper Sparrow
Savannah Sparrow
Western Meadowlark
Brown-headed Cowbird

Birds Associated with a Subalpine Meadow (open, sometimes wet meadows or parklands)

Swainson's Hawk
Peregrine Falcon
Sandhill Crane
Great Horned Owl

Common Raven
Mountain Bluebird
Vesper Sparrow
Savannah Sparrow

Birds Associated with Willow (areas dominated by Willow or Willow-Sedge)

Swainson's Hawk
Sora
Common Snipe
Common Raven
Yellow Warbler
Common Yellowthroat

Wilson's Warbler
Chipping Sparrow
Lincoln's Sparrow
White-crowned Sparrow

Birds Associated with Lodgepole Pine

Swainson's Hawk
Red-tailed Hawk
Cooper's Hawk
Sharp-shinned Hawk
Ruffed Grouse
Great Gray Owl
Williamson's Sapsucker
Hairy Woodpecker
Three-toed Woodpecker
Northern Flicker
Gray Jay
Steller's Jay
Clark's Nutcracker
Common Raven

Mountain Chickadee
Red-breasted Nuthatch
Ruby-crowned Kinglet
Mountain Bluebird
Townsend's Solitaire
Swainson's Thrush
Hermit Thrush
American Robin
Yellow-rumped Warbler
Chipping Sparrow
Dark-eyed Junco
Cassin's Finch
Red Crossbill
Pine Siskin

Birds Associated with Subalpine Fir (areas dominated by Subalpine fir and/or whitebark pine)

Swainson's Hawk
Northern Goshawk
Blue Grouse
Hairy Woodpecker
Steller's Jay
Gray Jay
Clark's Nutcracker
Common Raven
Mountain Chickadee
Red-breasted Nuthatch
Ruby-crowned Kinglet
Mountain Bluebird

Townsend's Solitaire
Hermit Thrush
American Robin
Yellow-rumped Warbler
White-crowned Sparrow
Dark-eyed Junco
Cassin's Finch
Red Crossbill
Pine Siskin

Birds Associated with Spruce-Fir (areas consisting of Englemann spruce and subalpine fir)

Cooper's Hawk
Northern Goshawk
Blue Grouse
Northern Pygmy Owl
Hairy Woodpecker
Black-backed Woodpecker
Three-toed Woodpecker
Steller's Jay
Clark's Nutcracker
Common Raven
Mountain Chickadee
Red-breasted Nuthatch
Brown Creeper
Golden-crowned Kinglet
Ruby-crowned Kinglet

Mountain Bluebird
Townsend's Solitaire
Hermit Thrush
American Robin
Yellow-rumped Warbler
Townsend's Warbler
Lincoln's Sparrow
White-crowned Sparrow
Dark-eyed Junco
Pine Grosbeak
Cassin's Finch
Red Crossbill
Pine Siskin

Birds Associated with Yellowstone Lake

Common Loon
Eared Grebe
Western Grebe
American White Pelican
Double-crested Cormorant
Trumpeter Swan
Canada Goose
Green-winged Teal
Mallard
Lesser Scaup
Barrow's Goldeneye
Common Merganser
Osprey

Bald Eagle
Killdeer
American Avocet
Willet
Spotted Sandpiper
Ring-billed Gull
California Gull
Caspian Tern
Common Tern
Forster's Tern
Belted Kingfisher
Bank Swallow
Cliff Swallow
Common Raven

Birds Associated with the Yellowstone River (above Upper Falls)

American White Pelican
Trumpeter Swan
Canada Goose
Green-winged Teal
Mallard
Blue-winged Teal
Cinnamon Teal
Northern Pintail
Northern Shoveler

Common Merganser
Osprey
Bald Eagle
Peregrine Falcon
Sandhill Crane
Killdeer
Spotted Sandpiper
Common Snipe
California Gull

Gadwall	Belted Kingfisher
Lesser Scaup	Bank Swallow
Ring-necked Duck	Cliff Swallow
Barrow's Goldeneye	Common Raven
Bufflehead	

Habitats Of The Alpine Zone

Birds Associated with the Alpine Environment (rugged, barren, treeless terrain consisting of rocks, sedges, and grasses)

Golden Eagle	Rock Wren
Peregrine Falcon	Mountain Bluebird
Prairie Falcon	Water Pipit
Horned Lark	White-crowned Sparrow
Clark's Nutcracker	Rosy Finch
Common Raven	

Feathers Beside the Thermal Areas.   One of the main reasons Yellowstone was set aside as a national park was because of its unique thermal features. Thermal features are simply hot water or steam features that appear on the surface of the earth. They result when heated magma and ground water, primarily from rain and snow, come in contact with one-another. Geologists estimate that there are up to 10,000 thermal features in Yellowstone. Even though thermal features are found throughout the Park, they are more concentrated in areas of high thermal activity called geyser basins. It is these unique forms of geothermal activ-

Dead male Williamson's Sapsucker—a victim of the thermal areas

ity (hot springs, geysers, fumaroles, solfataras, and mud-pots), along with an abundance of wildlife in a wilderness environment, that has given Yellowstone the reputation as one of the foremost natural attractions in the world.

Geyser basins and hot springs areas create openings in a predominantly forested environment, thus attracting a variety of wildlife. Because of the heat created by the geo-thermal areas, food is available for longer periods of time. Water courses closely associated with these areas remain open throughout the winter months. Birds, as well as mammals and insects, are attracted to these areas because they provide food, shelter, and warmth during cold periods.

Thermal features are not always beneficial to birds, and in some instances they may be fatal. During spring and fall migration, small birds are forced to seek food and shelter, particularly during severe storms. The small caves and gas vents found around hot springs and geyser basins are attractive to many of the smaller migratory birds. But some of these small caves and gas vents contain high concentrations of carbon dioxide, which displace the oxygen in the air. The hapless birds quickly die, primarily from suffocation. Thousands of birds have died over the years by seeking the shelter of these deadly caves and gas vents, but only a small fraction of Yellowstone's birds die in this manner.

The remains of the victims disappear quite rapidly, due to accelerated decomposition created by the sulfurous acid in the gas. Sometimes all that can be found are "feathers beside the thermal areas."

Some birds associated with the thermal areas in the Summer include: Killdeer, Hairy Woodpecker, Northern Flicker, Tree Swallow, Clark's Nutcracker, Common Raven, Red-breasted Nuthatch, Mountain Bluebird, Yellow-rumped Warbler, Chipping Sparrow, Dark-eyed Junco, Red Crossbill, and Pine Siskin.

THE SEASONS
Even greater than the changes the visitor encounters in traveling between Yellowstone's life-zones are the environmental changes brought about by the seasons. Yellowstone in winter is an altogether different world than Yellowstone in July. And each season presents the serious birder with a unique set of challenges and opportunities.

The Summer Breeding Season   Most people visit Yellowstone in the summer. Therefore, this book is geared more specifically to the summer months. But the short summer season is also important because it is the peak period for breeding birds, the season of the greatest abundance of birds, and the season when the greatest diversity of birds occurs.

Here are some time periods I would recommend for experiencing specific summer birding events in Yellowstone:

FOR THE GREATEST DIVERSITY OF BIRDS: early June to mid-July, and mid-August to mid-September

FOR THE PEAK OF THE NESTING SEASON: early June to mid-July

FOR THE GREATEST NUMBERS OF BIRDS: mid-July to early September

FOR THE PEAK OF BIRD SONG ACTIVITY: late May to early July

In the spring, as the length of the days increases, the hormonal activity in birds is stimulated. In the late spring, birds begin setting up nesting territories, which can be defended physically, visually, or through sound. Bird songs are used not only to attract a mate or to communicate, but also to advertise a territory. Birds sing more in the early morning than during other parts of the day. The timing of the breeding season for birds is closely tied to the hours of sunlight in a day, known as the photoperiod. The longest period of light or the longest day of the year occurs during the summer solstice, June 21/June 22. As the length of daylight decreases and as the nestlings get older, bird song activity quickly decreases.

The longest days of the year also offer the most ideal conditions for bird nesting, brooding, and rearing, in the form of optimum weather, greatest diversity of available vegetation, and greatest diversity of available food.

Spring and Fall Bird Migration.   Not all birds in Yellowstone migrate, but migration does play a very important role in the distribution, ecology, and perpetuity of Yellowstone birds. Migration is defined as the regular, extensive, seasonal movement of birds between their breeding area and their wintering area. Of the 160 species of birds that are known to nest in Yellowstone National Park, approximately one-fourth remain in Yellowstone as year-round residents. All the other species must migrate to other areas to overwinter.

It is the migratory aspect of birds that truly identifies the resources of Yellowstone National Park and other areas as international resources. The Swainson's Hawk for example, migrates from its summer range the open meadows of Yellowstone National Park to its wintering range the pampas of Argentina. Some Trumpeter Swans on the other hand migrate from their summer range on lakes in western Canada such as Nahanni National Park to their wintering range, the geothermal influenced waters of Yellowstone National Park. Some Semipalmated Sandpipers use specific mudflats in Yellowstone, from year to year as key stop over areas enroute from their summer range in the arctic tundra of North America to their wintering range on the coastal beaches of South America. All of these diverse environments play an important role in the survival and perpetuation of migratory birds.

Birds are forced to migrate for different reasons, but food and weather undoubtedly play a vital role. However they do not provide the total reasons for migration. Warblers, for example, move south long before they have to, whereas many species of ducks do not move until ice and snow become so severe that it forces them to leave. Storms sometimes put migrating birds in places they haven't been before. Birds that are unusual for a particular area typically show up during migration, which are usually periods of unsettled weather.

Each group of birds migrates differently. Most species are gregarious during migration, but the degree of social interaction and flocking behavior varies accordingly. The characteristic V-shaped flocks of Canada Geese and Tundra Swans best typify bird migration. However other birds migrate quite differently. Red-winged Blackbirds migrate in large flocks resembling storm clouds, American White Pelicans move in synchronous choreographed pods, Semipalmated Sandpipers reel in energized coordinated flights, and Common Nighthawks wander in erratic loose aggregations. Raptors on the other hand migrate in a number of different ways; some travel alone, some in pairs, others in groups referred to as kettles consisting of the same species or a mixture of species.

Different groups of birds migrate at different hours of the day. Ducks, geese, and swans migrate both day and night. Hawks, eagles, and cranes migrate during the day. Small songbirds such as warblers, on the other hand, migrate at night. For many birds, nighttime is usually the safest time to avoid predators and weather conditions are much more stable at this time.

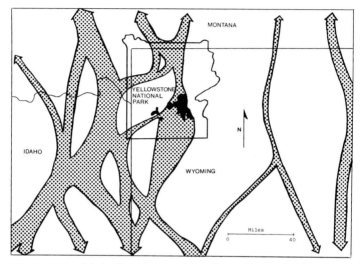

Fig. 9. Major bird migration corridors in and around Yellowstone National Park.

Different groups of birds migrate at different altitudes and at different speeds. Most migrant birds fly within 3000 feet of the ground. Those species that migrate at night are found migrating much closer to the ground. Warblers are an excellent example of a night migrant that flies close to the ground. Oftentimes they are found flying through or barely above the vegetation, which most often is within 50 feet of the ground. Waterfowl migrate at night at higher elevations than warblers and even higher elevations during the day. Most birds migrate at speeds between 20 and 55 miles per hour. There is a great deal of variation in migration speeds of birds between and amongst species, at different altitudes, and with different weather conditions.

In northern North America most migratory bird species move south in the autumn and usually take a slow, less direct route to get there. In the spring most migrant birds

YELLOWSTONE'S ENVIRONMENTS

that are heading north move quite rapidly and travel in more direct, broad paths or fronts. Yellowstone happens to lie adjacent to one of the most important migratory bird corridors in this section of mountainous western North America, known as the Snake River-Missouri River corridor. Millions of birds travel through this migratory corridor and other small migratory corridors on their way to and from nesting and wintering areas. Birds from nesting areas as far away as Alaska, and wintering areas as far away as South America funnel through this area. The Snake River-Missouri River migratory corridor, is located just west of Yellowstone National Park (Figure 9).

Besides the typical north-south migration of birds in and around Yellowstone, there is another type of migration found almost exclusively in mountainous environments. This movement of birds up and down mountains is called altitudinal migration. In almost all cases, birds that are found in Yellowstone as year round residents are forced to move down to lower elevations in the winter due to severe weather and shortages of food. The exception to this rule is the Blue Grouse, which actually winters at higher elevations primarily along windswept ridges feeding on buds and needles of trees. Not all migrant birds move in a north-south direction in North America. Some birds like eagles and falcons may wander at random and have been found at times to move in an east-west direction especially after nesting. Red Crossbills incidently are nomadic irregular wanderers whose movements are influenced by the state of their conifer cone crop supply. Bird migration is one of those complex natural phenomena that poses so many questions it may never be totally understood. There have been a number of theories that partially explain why birds migrate but no single explanation adequately answers the all important question of why birds migrate. The weakness is that theories can only explain bird migration for a limited number of species and fail to explain the bird migration phenomenon as a whole. Bird navigation is also a very complex phenomenon. Some birds use mountain ranges, rivers, and other natural landmarks as guiding lines during migration. Various studies have shown that some birds migrate by using the sun, others the stars, some by the earth's magnetic field, some by gravity, perhaps all of these factors combined.

The best time to observe bird migration in Yellowstone is in late summer to early fall, usually from mid-August to early November. Spring migration is not as spectacular as the fall migration in Yellowstone because many of the bird migrants bypass Yellowstone to avoid the late snowmelt and the large amount of snow still on the ground. If, however, one would like to plan a spring trip to Yellowstone, the best time to observe spring bird migration would be from late April to early June.

Winter. Yellowstone is a winter wonderland. In the winter, however, the birdlife is quite limited due to extremely harsh weather conditions. The weather is so severe that only 42 species of birds, or 23 percent, remain in Yellowstone year round. Another 7 species of birds are regularly found in Yellowstone only in the winter. These migratory birds nest in the more northerly latitudes and winter in the United States. The greatest diversity of wintering birds in Yellowstone is found at lower elevations where the weather conditions are mildest—in particular, in the area around Mammoth.

Traveling in the Winter. Throughout the rest of Yellowstone, birds are sparsely distributed in the winter. Places where birds do concentrate in this heavy snow country are mainly areas with open water, big game wintering areas, or thermal areas. Travel in the winter can be difficult. However, the road from Mammoth to Cooke City is maintained by snow plows, so vehicles can pass year round. In the winter the best roads to travel by automobile for bird watching are: Gardiner to Mammoth, Mammoth to Tower Junction, and Tower Junction to Cooke City. Throughout the Park, snowmobiles, snow coaches, and cross-country skiing are the major modes of winter transportation. The best routes to travel for bird watching in the winter, using these specialized modes of transportation, are: West Yellowstone to Madison, Madison to Old Faithful, and Canyon to Fishing Bridge (Figure 10).

Annual Audubon Christmas Bird Count. The Mammoth area, because of its mild winter weather, diversity of environments, and diversity of birdlife, is one of the many sites of the National Audubon Society's Annual Christmas Bird Counts conducted in North America. The first Christmas Bird count was conducted by Dr. Frank Chapman in the early 1900's in the eastern United States. Since that time, thousands of bird watchers have participated in the annual event nationwide. The Christmas Bird Count is a one day count, conducted some time during the last two weeks of December and the first week in January. The dates of the Mammoth count vary from year to year. Anyone is invited to participate in this activity. Information concerning the Audubon Christmas Bird Count in Yellowstone is usually available in early December by writing: Research Division, Yellowstone National Park, Wyoming 82190.

Black-billed Magpie on a bighorn sheep lamb's head

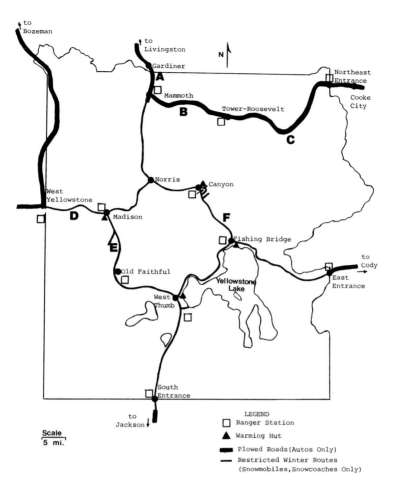

Fig. 10. Access to Yellowstone in Winter.

Races of Dark-eyed Juncos found in Yellowstone, from left to right: Pink-sided; Slate-colored; Montana-Oregon

YELLOWSTONE'S ENVIRONMENTS

Some Birds Likely to be Encountered
on a Winter Trip to Yellowstone

Species	Area A	B	C	D	E	F
Great Blue Heron				x	x	
Trumpeter Swan				x		x
Tundra Swan				x	x	
Canada Goose				x	x	
Mallard	x			x		x
Common Goldeneye	x		x	x		x
Barrow's Goldeneye	x		x	x		x
Common Merganser	x		x	x	x	x
Bald Eagle	x	x	x		x	
Northern Goshawk		x	x		x	
Golden Eagle	x	x	x			
Blue Grouse		x	x			
Ruffed Grouse		x	x			
Common Snipe	x				x	
Great Horned Owl	x	x			x	
Northern Pygmy-Owl	x	x	x			
Belted Kingfisher	x			x	x	
Hairy Woodpecker	x	x				
Downy Woodpecker	x					
Three-toed Woodpecker	x	x				
Steller's Jay		x	x	x		x
Gray Jay					x	x
Clark's Nutcracker	x	x	x	x	x	x
Black-billed Magpie	x	x				
Clark's Nutcracker	x	x	x	x	x	x
Common Raven	x	x	x	x	x	x
Black-capped Chickadee	x					
Mountain Chickadee	x	x	x	x	x	x
American Dipper	x	x	x	x	x	x
Red-breasted Nuthatch	x	x	x		x	
White-breasted Nuthatch	x	x				
Brown Creeper	x	x				
Townsend's Solitaire	x	x	x			
Bohemian Waxwing	x	x				
Northern Shrike	x		x			

Species	Area	A	B	C	D	E	F
American Tree Sparrow		x	x				
Rosy Finch		x	x	x			
Pine Grosbeak			x		x	x	x
Red Crossbill			x	x	x	x	x
Common Redpoll		x		x			

Clark's Nutcracker on a bison horn

3

THE CHARACTERISTIC
BIRDS OF YELLOWSTONE

Of THE MANY INTERESTING AND CHARACTER-
istic bird species in Yellowstone National Park, the following twenty species have been selected for a more
detailed treatment in the following "profiles." Although
some of these species are common and conspicuous and
some are secretive and rare, a birder will have a fairly good
chance of encountering most of these birds during a summer visit to the park. I have chosen to call them the "characteristic" birds of Yellowstone because, to me, they are
the birds that best typify what is unique about Yellowstone environments and also have a strong appeal to the
general public. The identification features presented in
this chapter are geared for the beginning birder. Inter-
mediate and advanced birders interested in more detailed
identification features are encouraged to consult a major
bird identification guide.

In reading through these bird profiles, you will undoubtedly come to a better understanding of birds as species
with specific habitat requirements. It is the big ecological
picture that is the most important experience – the interrelationships that the landscape, the weather, the habitat,
the plant life, and the animal life have with Yellowstone
birds and the role that birds have in the Yellowstone
ecosystem.

The key headings under each of the twenty characteristic birds of Yellowstone are self explanatory and warrant no
further clarification. However, bird abundance, as difficult
as it is to explain, can be confusing if it is not defined. The

following categories of *"Overall Abundance"* are as follows:

Abundant: Can be encountered without much effort in the appropriate habitat.

Common: Can be encountered in the appropriate habitat but may require some effort in looking and/or listening.

Uncommon: These birds are not encountered everyday, but one or more sightings are possible if one spends several days of diligent searching in the appropriate habitat.

Rare: Seldom encountered by park visitors who are experienced birders; one will need luck as well as good eyes to find this species, even in the appropriate habitat.

● Occasionally observed during the month.

Note: All photos of birds in this book are of adults only. For immature plumages, juvenal plumages, plumage variations, morphological color phases, etc., consult a major bird identification guide.

Photo by Michael Quinton.

COMMON LOON
(*Gavia immer*)

IDENTIFICATION FEATURES
1. Black head, black and white checkered body.
2. Heavy, black, pointed bill.
3. Low profile in water.
4. Larger than a Mallard.
5. Sexes have similar plumage.

POSSIBLE IDENTIFICATION CONFUSION:
Double-crested Cormorant: large black bird with hooked bill and long tail. Male Common Merganser: Large black and white bird, black head & back, white breast and flanks, red bill and feet.

MONTHLY OCCURRENCE

J	F	M	A	M	J	J	A	S	O	N	D

Best months for observation: May, September, and October.

LIFE ZONES

Foothills	Montane	Subalpine	Alpine
	———————————	

HABITAT
Water: sometimes large marshes; large, slow-flowing rivers; more commonly found on mountain lakes.

BEST OBSERVATION POINTS
3   Steamboat Point-Sedge Bay
4   Mary Bay

BEST GENERAL AREA
Yellowstone Lake

CHANCES OF FINDING THE COMMON LOON IN YELLOWSTONE
Hard to see, easy to hear. Result: moderate chance.

POPULATION STATUS
Variable (minor population fluctuations from year to year).

OVERALL ABUNDANCE
U   Uncommon. Less than fifteen pairs of common loons nest in Yellowstone. During migration, in May and in September to October, hundreds of Common Loons are found in the Park, but because their numbers are so low in the summer, they are regarded as uncommon.

NESTS AND NESTING
Nesting evidence is well established. Common Loons nest on large lakes in summer. They build their nests, which consist of a mass of reeds on or near the shore, in late May to mid-June, when newly hatched Canada Goose goslings appear. Common Loons lay one to three eggs, normally two. Young loons (loonlets) fledge in mid- to late September, usually at about the time bull elk are bugling.

FOODS AND FEEDING
Food is primarily fish, although diet varies with locale.

Common Loons dive for food from a floating position on the water's surface.

MOVEMENTS AND WINTERING
Common Loons are found singly or in pairs. They are sometimes found on the Yellowstone River prior to ice-out on Yellowstone Lake, and they stay in Yellowstone until Yellowstone Lake freezes. In winter they migrate to open water, usually large inland lakes or coastal areas free of ice. They are found at lower elevations during migration.

INTERESTING FACTS
The genus *Gavia* is derived from the family Gaviidae, which includes the loons and divers. The word *immer* means plunge or dive. Loons are excellent swimmers, but on land they are very cumbersome. The North American name "loon" is supposedly derived from *lómr*, a Scandinavian word meaning an awkward person. Only in North America are they called loons; throughout the rest of the northern hemisphere they are called "divers"—in Great Britain *Gavia immer* is commonly called the Great Northern Diver. For readers familiar with the north woods, the haunting, yodel-like call of the loon is the sound of solitude, the wail of the wilderness.

VISITOR CAUTION
Nesting loons are extremely sensitive to human disturbance.

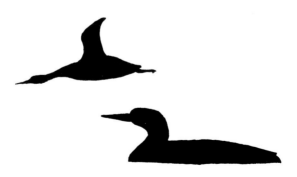

COMMON LOON   47

Photo by Terry McEneaney.

AMERICAN WHITE PELICAN
(Pelecanus erythrorhynchos)

IDENTIFICATION FEATURES
1. Very large white bird with massive orange or yellow bill.
2. Black wing tips (primarily and secondary feathers), obvious in flight.
3. Large gular (throat) pouch.
4. High profile in water.
5. Characteristic flapping and gliding flight; mid-day soaring.
6. Sexes similar.

POSSIBLE IDENTIFICATION CONFUSION
Trumpeter Swan: all white, with black bill and feet.

MONTHLY OCCURRENCE

J	F	M	A	M	J	J	A	S	O	N	D
				▬	▬	▬	▬	▬	▬		

Best months for observation: May and June.

LIFE ZONES

Foothills Montane Subalpine Alpine

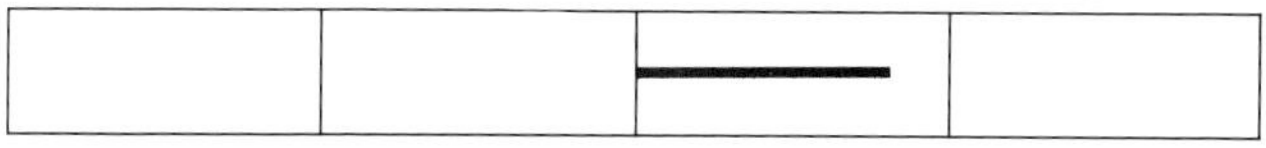

HABITAT

Water: shallow wate[illegible] lakes or large slow-flowing rivers; more commo[illegible]nd on Yellowstone Lake and north along the Yellowstone River to Hayden Valley.

BEST OBSERVATION POINTS

8 Fishing Bridge

11 Wildlife Overlook

BEST GENERAL AREA

Yellowstone Lake

Yellowstone River near Hayden Valley

CHANCES OF FINDING THE AMERICAN WHITE PELICAN IN YELLOWSTONE

Easy to see, hard to hear. Result: moderate chance.

POPULATION STATUS

Highly variable (population fluctuations from year to year are the result of fluctuating water levels on Yellowstone Lake).

OVERALL ABUNDANCE

C Common. Approximately two to four hundred pairs of American White Pelicans nest in Yellowstone. The overall YNP population during optimum years can reach as high as one thousand pelicans.

NESTS AND NESTING

Nesting evidence is well established. American White Pelicans nest in colonies, known as rookeries, which are restricted to small islands on Yellowstone Lake. The nest is nothing more than a simple circular scrape in gravel, sometimes intermixed with loose plant material. Where they nest on sandy soils, these scrapes may be slightly elevated, forming small circular mounds. Nest building and egg laying are nearly simultaneous and occur in early to mid-May, at about the time bison calves are born. Pelicans lay two to three eggs, normally two. Young pelicans fledge in early to late August, usually around the time when Brown-headed Cowbirds are congregating in large flocks.

FOODS AND FEEDING
The food of the pelican is exclusively fish. American White Pelicans do not dive for their food, but rather catch fish on or near the surface by swimming or wading in shallow water. Pelicans feed in flocks and together force fish to be trapped in shallow water. They use their expandable gular pouches mainly as dip nets for catching fish. They keep the fish in their pouches only long enough to let the water drain out, then they swallow the fish whole.

MOVEMENTS AND WINTERING
Pelicans are commonly found in flocks (usually greater than two individuals). A primary migratory staging area for Yellowstone's American White Pelicans is the Great Salt Lake in Utah. Yellowstone's pelicans are known to winter on the coastal lowlands of Mexico.

INTERESTING FACTS
Erythrorhynchos is a Greek word meaning red snout. The pelican is renowned for its famous limerick: "A wonderful bird is a pelican/ It eats more food than its belly can/ Hold in its beak enough for a week/And I don't know how the hell he can." White Pelicans can hold up to three gallons in their gular pouch, which is nearly three times the capacity of the stomach. However, the limerick exaggerates—a pelican *cannot* hold in its beak enough for a week!

Pelicans were observed in Yellowstone even by some of the earliest explorers. J. Davis, a member of the Stuart party in 1863, shot a pelican at the mouth of a creek that is today known as Pelican Creek.

VISITOR CAUTION
The nesting islands are closed to the public. A high mortality of young occurs when the nesting colonies are disturbed by humans.

AMERICAN WHITE PELICAN 51

TRUMPETER SWAN
(Cygnus buccinator)

IDENTIFICATION FEATURES
1. Very large white bird with black bill and feet.
2. All white wings.
3. Young (cygnets) have grayish plumage.
4. Call resembles French taxi-cab horn.
5. Sexes similar

POSSIBLE IDENTIFICATION CONFUSION
Summer: American White Pelican: distinctive black primaries and secondaries on wings; large orange bill and pouch.
Winter: Tundra Swan: smaller size; yellow spot in front of eye (not always present); round head.
Spring and fall: Snow goose: black primaries on wings.

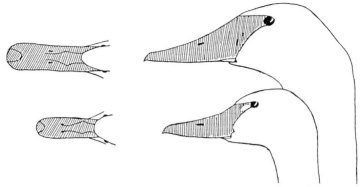

Head comparisons of Trumpeter Swan (above) and Tundra Swan (below)

MONTHLY OCCURRENCE

J	F	M	A	M	J	J	A	S	O	N	D

Best months for observation: February, June, July, and November.

LIFE ZONES

	Foothills	Montane	Subalpine	Alpine
Summer		———————————	
Winter	———————————		

HABITAT
Water: lakes, ponds, marshes, and large slow-flowing rivers with an abundance of submergent vegetation.

BEST OBSERVATION POINTS
 4   Mary Bay
56   Seven Mile Bridge

BEST GENERAL AREA
Madison River

CHANCES OF FINDING THE
TRUMPETER SWAN IN YELLOWSTONE
Easy to see, easy to hear. Result: excellent chance.

POPULATION STATUS
Resident population decreasing, migratory population increasing.

OVERALL ABUNDANCE

C   Common. Less than fifteen pairs of Trumpeter Swans nest in Yellowstone. From May to September the population rarely exceeds forty individuals. From October to April the population increases, mainly due to an influx of migrants from the north. Population figures fluctuate from forty to several hundred individuals throughout the winter. Swans at this time of year are found mainly on the Yellowstone and Madison rivers.

NESTS AND NESTING

Nesting evidence is well established. A Trumpeter Swan nest consists of a large, floating mass of emergent vegetation. They build their nests at about the time bison calves are born, in early to mid-May. They lay four to six eggs, normally five. Cygnets fledge in late September to early October, usually at about the time bull elk are bugling.

FOODS AND FEEDING

Diet consists primarily of submergent vegetation and aquatic invertebrates. The swans prefer shallow, calm, or slow-moving water for feeding, and they feed by dipping their heads under water.

MOVEMENTS AND WINTERING

Trumpeter Swans are commonly found in the summer in pairs or in pairs with gray cygnets. In the winter, during stressful periods, Trumpeter Swans become more sociable and gather into large flocks. Yellowstone's resident adult swans do not move very far in the winter—their movements can best be described as nomadic, as they wander around looking for open water areas where food is available. In the winter, Yellowstone's swan population is composed of both nomadic residents and migrants.

INTERESTING FACTS

Cygnus is a Latin word meaning swan, while *buccinator* means bugler or trumpeter. The Trumpeter Swan gets its name from its trumpet-like call. It is regarded as the largest of all North American wildfowl. John James Audubon cherished the primary feather of the Trumpeter Swan as one of the best quill pens for writing. The Trumpeter Swan was never classified as an endangered species; however, in the 1930s less than one hundred were believed to exist in the world. With the advent of the airplane, a sizeable population was discovered in Alaska in the 1950s. The wild Trumpeter Swan is found only in North America. Today, due to conservation efforts, approximately ten thousand swans are known to exist—over eight thousand are found in Alaska alone. Recent problems with Trumpeter Swan reproduction and lead poisoning have threatened the regional population. The regional summer Trumpeter Swan population is currently less than five hundred individuals. In the winter, due to the influx of migrants from northern latitudes, the regional population can be as high as fifteen hundred individuals. The male swan is called a cob, the female a pen, and young swans are called cygnets.

VISITOR CAUTION
Trumpeter Swans have a high incidence of nest failure during the critical incubation and brooding periods. The public is asked to exercise extreme caution when viewing nesting swans.

Photo by Michael Quinton.

HARLEQUIN DUCK
(Histrionicus histrionicus)

IDENTIFICATION FEATURES
1. Male: small, gray bill; gray-purple plumage; white markings on head, breast, and back; chestnut color on head and flanks (complex pattern, see photograph or field guides).
2. Female: small gray bill; brown plumage; two to three white spots on head, one of which is behind the eye.
3. Smaller than a Mallard.

POSSIBLE IDENTIFICATION CONFUSION
Female Bufflehead: dark brown head with long white cheek patch below and behind the eye.

MONTHLY OCCURRENCE

J	F	M	A	M	J	J	A	S	O	N	D
									•	•	

Best months for observation: May and June.

LIFE ZONES

Foothills	Montane	Subalpine	Alpine

HABITAT
Water: rapids, fast-moving water, cascading creeks and rivers.

BEST OBSERVATIONS POINTS   BEST GENERAL AREA
10   LeHardy Rapids   Yellowstone River
27   Yellowstone Bridge

CHANCES OF FINDING THE
HARLEQUIN DUCK IN YELLOWSTONE
Hard to see, hard to hear. Result: difficult chance.

POPULATION STATUS
Variable (minor population fluctuations from year to year).

OVERALL ABUNDANCE
R   Rare. Relatively little is known about the Harlequin Duck in Yellowstone. Population estimate is less than twenty nesting pairs. Because of the low population estimate and its secretive habits, this species is regarded as rare.

NESTS AND NESTING
Nesting evidence is fairly well established. The Harlequin Duck nests along fast-moving creeks and rivers, usually in an alcove of a cutbank, among exposed roots or trees, or sometimes in floodwater debris. The nest is simply lined with grasses. Nesting and incubation occurs in mid-May to late June and coincides with the peak spring floodwater

runoff. They lay five to ten eggs, usually seven. Young Harlequins fledge in late August to mid-September, around the time bull elk are first heard bugling.

FOODS AND FEEDING
The Harlequin Duck's food requirements in Yellowstone are very similar to those of the American Dipper, namely aquatic invertebrates found in fast-flowing water. The aquatic life stages of caddisflies, mayflies, stoneflies, and blackflies are preferred. The duck feeds by diving from a floating position on the water's turbulent surface, and it is also capable of walking underwater, using its wings sometimes for balance. It feeds usually facing upstream and works the spaces between river rocks for insects.

MOVEMENTS AND WINTERING
The adult male Harlequin is unique in that it abandons the female sometime when she is incubating to make its journey to the Pacific coast. Once the young have fledged, the adult female escorts them on their long migration along the large rivers to the Pacific coast. Pairs reunite on the wintering grounds and return to Yellowstone in the spring to complete the cycle.

INTERESTING FACTS
Histrionicus is a Latin word meaning a stage player or actor. This duck's common name refers to the showy plumage of the male, which resembles Harlequin, the colorfully-clad character of Italian comedy and pantomime. The male is called a lord, the female a lady. The male Harlequin, as colorful as he seems, is sometimes difficult to discern in fast-moving water and often is overlooked because in direct sunlight he appears to be a shiny rock.

HARLEQUIN DUCK

Photo by John Good, courtesy of the National Park Service.

BARROW'S GOLDENEYE
(Bucephala islandica)

IDENTIFICATION FEATURES
1. Male: black head with white crescent in front of yellow eye; black back with white spots on scapulars; white underparts.
2. Female: Brown head, gray body, yellow eye.
3. Stubby, triangular bill, steep forehead.
4. Smaller than a Mallard.

POSSIBLE IDENTIFICATION CONFUSION
Common Goldeneye: male has a round white spot in front of the eye, more white on scapulars; both sexes have a sloping forehead. (See field guides for differences in bill color.)

MONTHLY OCCURRENCE

J	F	M	A	M	J	J	A	S	O	N	D

Best months for observation: June, July, and October.

LIFE ZONES

	Foothills	Montane	Subalpine	Alpine
Summer			▬▬▬▬	
Winter		▬▬▬▬▬▬		

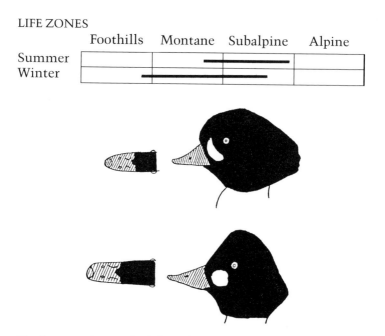

Head comparisons of adult male Goldeneyes: Barrow's (above) and Common (below)

Head comparisons of adult female Goldeneyes: Barrow's (left) and Common (right)

HABITAT
Water: lakes and larger rivers.

BEST OBSERVATION POINTS
1   Sylvan Lake
8   Fishing Bridge

BEST GENERAL AREA
Yellowstone Lake
also along the Yellowstone
River to Hayden Valley

CHANCES OF FINDING THE BARROW'S
GOLDENEYE IN YELLOWSTONE
Easy to see, easy to hear. Result: excellent chance.

POPULATION STATUS
Variable (minor population fluctuations from year to year).

OVERALL ABUNDANCE
A   Abundant. Hundreds of Barrow's Goldeneyes are found
in Yellowstone in the summer, and it is the most fre-
quently seen goldeneye. In winter, however, Common
Goldeneyes far outnumber Barrow's Goldeneyes in
Yellowstone.

NESTS AND NESTING
Nesting evidence is well established. The nest is a cavity
in a tree, lined with wood chips and down, usually on or
near the shores of a lake. Barrow's Goldeneyes choose their
nest cavity and lay eggs in late May to early June, about the
time willows are beginning to leaf out. They lay six to fifteen eggs, normally ten. Young goldeneyes fledge from late
June to early July, usually about the time cutthroat trout
are spawning on Yellowstone Lake.

FOODS AND FEEDING
The food of the goldeneye is primarily small fish, although
invertebrates and submergent vegetation are also important. They dive for food from a floating position on the
water's surface.

MOVEMENTS AND WINTERING
In the summer Barrow's Goldeneyes are often found in
pairs or in pairs with young. As the winter progresses they
gather in large flocks, sometimes mixed with Common
Goldeneyes. In the winter, many Barrow's Goldeneyes
move to lower elevations, while some winter as far away
as the Pacific coast.

INTERESTING FACTS
Bucephala is a Greek word meaning "having a broad
forehead"; *islandica* is Latin and means of Iceland. The
shape of the Barrow's Goldeneye head is quite different

from that of the Common Goldeneye. Both species, however, have gold-colored eyes. The name Barrow is in honor of Sir John Barrow (1764-1848), a long-time promoter of arctic exploration and one of the founders of the Royal Geographic Society. Goldeneyes, once called whistle-winged ducks, produce a characteristic wing-sound in flight, audible from a great distance, which is the result of the vibration of the wing feathers.

Photo by Robert Twist.

OSPREY
(Pandion haliaetus)

IDENTIFICATION FEATURES
1. Very large bird, dark above, white below.
2. Long, narrow wings, swept back at wrists.
3. Dark patches at wrists, prominent in flight.
4. White head with dark brown eyestripe.
5. Frequently hovers over water before plunging feet-first for fish.
6. Sexes similar.

POSSIBLE IDENTIFICATION CONFUSION
Bald Eagle: white head, white tail, dark brown-black body.

MONTHLY OCCURRENCE

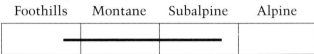

J	F	M	A	M	J	J	A	S	O	N	D

Best months for observation: June, July, and August.

LIFE ZONES

Foothills	Montane	Subalpine	Alpine

HABITAT
Water: lakes and rivers where there is an abundance of fish.
Open meadows should not be discounted, however.

BEST OBSERVATION POINTS   BEST GENERAL AREA
16   Artist Point   Grand Canyon of the
17   Lookout Point   Yellowstone

CHANCES OF FINDING THE OSPREY IN YELLOWSTONE
Easy to see, easy to hear. Result: excellent chance.

POPULATION STATUS
Variable (minor population fluctuations from year to year)
to increasing.

OVERALL ABUNDANCE
C   Common. Approximately fifty to sixty pairs of ospreys
nest in Yellowstone.

NESTS AND NESTING
Nesting evidence is well established. Nest consists of a
mass of large sticks, usually located on a rock pinnacle or
at the apex of a conifer. Ospreys lay two to four eggs, usually three. They normally begin incubating from mid- to
late May, which is about the time river otter kits are first
seen out of the den and accompanying the adults. Young
ospreys fledge in mid- to late August, usually at about the
time the grass in the subalpine meadows turns a golden
color.

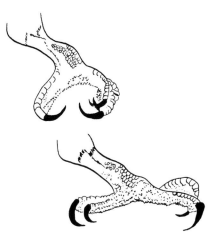

Osprey talons—and the reversible outer toe for catching fish

FOODS AND FEEDING

The food of the osprey is almost exclusively fish. Ospreys capture fish by diving into water either from a perch in a tree or from a hovering position over the water. The genus *Pandion* is uniquely equipped with a reversible outer toe, and the talons are of equal length, features that make it easier to catch fish. Ospreys also have spiny pads, or spicules, on the bottom of their feet, which aid in grasping slippery prey. When airborne, the osprey carries the fish head-first in its talons. This aerodynamic method is one way the osprey can carry off large-sized prey with a minimal amount of effort.

MOVEMENTS AND WINTERING

Ospreys are often found singly or in pairs. Band recoveries indicate that ospreys from the western states migrate south to winter along the Pacific coast of Central America. The young remain on the wintering grounds during the second summer, returning to Yellowstone as two-year olds.

INTERESTING FACTS

The word osprey means literally "feeds on the bones." The bones this refers to are the multitude of bones found in fish. The osprey, sometimes referred to as the fish hawk, belongs to a family of raptors (Pandionidae) that contains only this one species. The genus *Pandion* is found worldwide wherever there is a combination of open water and fish. The term *haliaetus* refers to fish eagles. Ospreys on Yellowstone Lake specialize on larger immature cutthroat trout for prey (eight to fourteen inches long). Other major predators on cutthroats (White Pelicans, Bald Eagles, Grizzly Bears) take mainly adult fish, whereas the much smaller immature cutthroat are consumed by Common Mergansers and Belted Kingfishers.

VISITOR CAUTION
Some nesting ospreys can be extremely sensitive to human disturbance, particularly during incubation and when nestlings are very young.

Photo by Frank Oberle

BALD EAGLE
(Haliaetus leucephalus)

IDENTIFICATION FEATURES
1. Adults: very large, brown-black birds with white head and short white tail.
2. Adults: massive yellow hooked beak, yellow eye.
3. Sexes similar.

POSSIBLE IDENTIFICATION CONFUSION
Golden Eagle: gray beak; golden-brown eye, golden-feathered nape; feathered legs. Please consult a field guide for greater details on separating the immature birds of these two species.

MONTHLY OCCURRENCE

J	F	M	A	M	J	J	A	S	O	N	D

Best months for observation: February, May, June, and December.

LIFE ZONES

	Foothills	Montane	Subalpine	Alpine
Summer			▬▬▬▬	
Winter	▬▬▬▬▬▬▬▬▬			

HABITAT

Water: primarily lakes, rivers, large creeks, and thermal areas bordering water; they periodically use open meadows.

BEST OBSERVATION POINTS
6   Pelican Creek Bridge
13   Alum Creek

BEST GENERAL AREA
Summer: Yellowstone Lake, Yellowstone River
Winter: Mammoth, Gardiner

CHANCES OF FINDING THE BALD EAGLE IN YELLOWSTONE

Easy to see, hard to hear. Result: moderate chance.

POPULATION STATUS

Variable (minor population fluctuations from year to year). Currently listed as an endangered species by the U.S. Fish and Wildlife Service.

OVERALL ABUNDANCE

U Uncommon. Approximately fifteen pairs of Bald Eagles nest in Yellowstone. Winter population figures rarely exceed thirty individuals.

NESTS AND NESTING

Nesting is well established. Bald Eagles nest along large lakes and rivers in Yellowstone. The nest consists of a mass of large sticks in a conifer. Egg laying occurs from late March to mid-April, when there is still deep snow in the Park. They lay one to three eggs, normally two. Eaglets fledge in late July to mid-August, about the time adult Canada Geese have completely molted their primary feathers and are able to fly once again.

FOODS AND FEEDING

Food in the summer is primarily fish and waterfowl, although a wide variety of food items have been documented. Waterfowl are easily taken during the molt, which is a flightless period in the summer when they shed their primary feathers. In the winter, Bald Eagles feed primarily on waterfowl and large ungulate carrion. They usually hunt from an elevated perch and sometimes locate food by closely watching the behavior of other predators and scavengers.

MOVEMENTS AND WINTERING
Some adult Bald Eagle pairs remain in Yellowstone year round, others move out of the Park to winter in areas where prey is more plentiful. Very few immature bald eagles winter within the Park. Some winter in areas adjacent to Yellowstone, while others migrate to the Pacific states (northern California to southern Washington).

INTERESTING FACTS
Sea and fish eagles are included in the genus *Haliaeetus.* The term *leucocephalus* is Greek and means "white head." Carolus Linnaeus is credited as the first person to name and classify the Bald Eagle. On June 20, 1782, the Bald Eagle was adopted as the national emblem of the United States. This eagle is called "bald" because of the white feathers on its head, which create a bald appearance.

The high elevation of Yellowstone National Park characteristically results in late spring snow melt, so the nesting chronology of Bald Eagles and other birdlife in the Park is similar to that of birds nesting in northern Canada.

VISITOR CAUTION
Nesting Bald Eagles are extremely sensitive to human disturbance.

Photo by Michael Quinton.

SWAINSON'S HAWK
(Buteo swainsonii)

IDENTIFICATION FEATURES
1. Long, narrow, pointed wings.
2. White underwing lining and dark flight features.
3. Long tail with several fine light and dark bands.
4. V-shaped (dihedral) wing profile in flight.
5. Plumage variable. Typical plumage consists of brown bib, white throat, and white belly; female: grey-brown (chocolate) breast; male: red-brown (chestnut) breast.
6. Size equal to that of a Mallard.

POSSIBLE IDENTIFICATION CONFUSION
Red-tailed Hawk: red tail, white breast and throat, dark head, and dark leading edge of wing.

Ferruginous Hawk: white "windows" on wings; wide gape extends past center of eye; yellow cere and gape lining.

MONTHLY OCCURRENCE

J	F	M	A	M	J	J	A	S	O	N	D

Best months for observation: June and July.

LIFE ZONES

Foothills	Montane	Subalpine	Alpine

HABITAT
Open areas: open meadows and the edge of open meadows, often bordered by aspen.

BEST OBSERVATION POINTS
11 Wildlife Overlook—Trout Creek
18 Cascade Meadows

BEST GENERAL AREA
Canyon Junction
Hayden Valley

CHANCES OF FINDING THE
SWAINSON'S HAWK IN YELLOWSTONE
Easy to see, hard to hear. Result: moderate chance.

POPULATION STATUS
Variable (minor population fluctuations from year to year).

OVERALL ABUNDANCE
C   Common. Less than eighty pairs of Swainson's Hawks nest in Yellowstone. Hundreds travel through Yellowstone during migration, which is during late April and late September. Since they are likely to be encountered on a trip to Yellowstone, they are considered common.

NESTS AND NESTING
Nesting evidence is well established. The flimsy stick nests, lined with aspen or willow leaves, are found in trees. Swainson's Hawks are nest building usually in late April to early May, about the time bison calves are born. They lay two to four eggs, normally two. Young hawks fledge in late July to early August, which coincides with the peak of thunderstorm activity in Yellowstone.

SWAINSON'S HAWK   71

FOODS AND FEEDING

Swainson's Hawks feed primarily on ground squirrels, although small birds and large insects are also taken. They hunt for prey by soaring or searching from an elevated perch.

MOVEMENTS AND WINTERING

Swainson's Hawks are often found singly or in pairs. Their annual arrival in and departure from Yellowstone is based on nature's clockwork and closely coincides with ground squirrel, small bird, and insect availability.

Swainson's Hawks migrate to South America in the winter, usually in large flocks, or "kettles." A vast majority of North American Swainson's Hawks winter on the pampas of Argentina.

INTERESTING FACTS

The genus *Buteo* is derived from Buteoninae, which is a subfamily of medium to large soaring hawks with broad wings and fairly short tails. The name Swainson, or *swainsonii*, honors William Swainson, an English ornithologist who was actively involved in North American ornithology in the 1800s. The Swainson's Hawk and the Peregrine Falcon are the only two North American raptors known to winter south of the Tropic of Capricorn in South America.

VISITOR CAUTION

Nesting Swainson's Hawks are extremely sensitive to human disturbance, particularly during the incubation period. Predators such as ravens will destroy unattended nests.

SWAINSON'S HAWK

Photo by Jerry Craig.

PEREGRINE FALCON
(Falco peregrinus)

IDENTIFICATION FEATURES
1. Long tail, pointed wings.
2. Black "helmet," and black wedge below eye.
3. Blue-gray back (races vary).
4. Slightly larger than a Rock Dove.
5. Sexes similar.

POSSIBLE IDENTIFICATION CONFUSION
Prairie Falcon: black "armpits," or axillars.

Prairie Falcon with black axillars ("armpits") under wings

Peregrine Falcon with uniform grey under wings.

MONTHLY OCCURRENCE

J	F	M	A	M	J	J	A	S	O	N	D
										•	

Best months for observation: May, June, July, and August.

LIFE ZONES

Foothills	Montane	Subalpine	Alpine

HABITAT
Water, open, and forested environments: lakes, rivers, pen meadows, large cliffs overlooking open meadows, and forested areas.

BEST OBSERVATION POINTS
12 Grizzly Overlook
13 Alum Creek

BEST GENERAL AREA
Hayden Valley

CHANCES OF FINDING THE
PEREGRINE FALCON IN YELLOWSTONE
Hard to see, hard to hear. Result: difficult chance.

POPULATION STATUS
Less than twelve Peregrine Falcons, which includes adults and immatures, are found in Yellowstone. The Peregrine Falcon is currently classified as an endangered species by the U.S. Fish and Wildlife Service.

OVERALL ABUNDANCE
R Rare. This is perhaps one of the rarest birds in Yellowstone. Efforts to release Peregrines back into the Yellowstone ecosystem are currently being conducted by the nonprofit Peregrine Fund (Boise, Idaho).

NESTS AND NESTING
Nesting evidence is well established. The nest consists of a simple scrape on a cliff ledge. Peregrines are egg laying in late April to mid-May, at about the time coyote pups are born. They lay three to four eggs. Young wild Peregrines fledge in early August, when other young fledgling birds become easy victims of prey.

FOODS AND FEEDING
In Yellowstone the Peregrine feeds primarily on waterfowl, songbirds, and shorebirds. It is an excellent hunter and dives at high speeds, striking its prey in mid-air.

MOVEMENTS AND WINTERING
Peregrines are most often observed singly or in pairs. They are known to winter along the coasts of the southern United States, Mexico, Central America, and South America. April to May and October to November seem to be the best times to observe migrating peregrines in Yellowstone.

PEREGRINE FALCON

INTERESTING FACTS

Falco means falcon, *peregrinus* means "wanderer" or "pilgrim." The Peregrine Falcon is reputed to be one of the fastest birds in the world. The normal cruising speed is from 40 to 55 miles per hour. The top speed of a Peregrine in a stoop or dive has been calculated to be as high as 238 miles per hour. Evidence clearly indicates that the use of DDT after World War II was responsible for the decline in the productivity of the Peregrine Falcon.

VISITOR CAUTION

Because Peregrines are one of the rarest species in Yellowstone, observers are cautioned against disturbing these birds and to watch them only from a distance.

Photo by Michael Quinton.

SANDHILL CRANE
(Grus canadensis)

IDENTIFICATION FEATURES
1. Tall, gray bird; long legs; long, straight neck.
2. Long, dark gray bill; red crown on gray head.
3. Flies with neck extended.
4. In flight, wing-beat has rapid up-stroke.
5. Call is a loud, rolling, musical rattle.
6. Sexes similar.

POSSIBLE IDENTIFICATION CONFUSION
Great Blue Heron: flies with neck folded; yellow bill;
white head with black stripe, gray neck.

MONTHLY OCCURRENCE

J	F	M	A	M	J	J	A	S	O	N	D

Best months for observation: May, June, and August.

LIFE ZONES

Foothills	Montane	Subalpine	Alpine

HABITAT
Open areas: preferably wet, sometimes dry, open meadows; also found in and on the edge of aspen groves, sparse willow stands, and lodgepole stands.

BEST OBSERVATION POINTS   BEST GENERAL AREA
11   Wildlife Overlook   Bechler, Fountain Flats
59   Fountain Flats

CHANCES OF FINDING THE
SANDHILL CRANE IN YELLOWSTONE
Hard to see, easy to hear. Result: moderate chance.

POPULATION STATUS
Variable (minor population fluctuations from year to year).

OVERALL ABUNDANCE
U   Uncommon. Less than sixty pairs of Sandhill Cranes nest in Yellowstone. Approximately two hundred cranes are found in the Park during peak population periods. Because they are scattered throughout the Park and are found in areas undisturbed by humans, they are regarded as uncommon.

NESTS AND NESTING
Nesting evidence is well established. A Sandhill Crane nest consists of elevated mounds of vegetation. The nest is commonly found in shallow wet meadows. They build their nests in late April to early May, when bison calves are

born. Sandhill Cranes lay one to three eggs, usually two. Young cranes fledge in late August to mid-September, when some aspen leaves are starting to turn gold.

FOODS AND FEEDING
The diet of the Sandhill Crane is diverse and consists of a variety of small insects, amphibians, rodents, grain, seeds, and roots. They are excellent walkers and feed by bending over and pecking at the ground with their bills.

MOVEMENTS AND WINTERING
Sandhill Cranes are often found in pairs or small flocks. During migration they are found in large flocks. Migrating cranes use two major staging areas en route to and from their wintering grounds: the Teton Basin area of Idaho and the San Luis Valley of Colorado. Sandhill Cranes from Yellowstone winter in the Rio Grande Valley of New Mexico and Mexico.

INTERESTING FACTS
Grus refers to the crane family and possibly to the guttural call that cranes make. The term "sandhill" refers to the sandhills of Nebraska, the heart of the prairie country and a fabulous area for migrating cranes.

One of the most spectacular of all bird behaviors is the crane's dance. This courting ritual involves primarily paired cranes, who quickly step around each other with wings half spread. Partners alternate as they leap high into the air with wings partially spread and legs held gracefully below the body. This behavior is interspersed with neck bowings and body stretchings. They often pick up sticks and pieces of grass and throw them up into the air, stabbing at them in the air as the objects come down. The call of the Sandhill Crane is one of the most primitive and eerie of all natural sounds. Many of the adult cranes in Yellowstone appear to have reddish-brown plumage, this cosmetic appearance results when the cranes spread reddish (iron oxide) soil on their plumage when the birds preen or trim their feathers.

VISITOR CAUTION
Since Sandhill Cranes are ground-nesting birds, human

scent near the nest can attract mammalian predators, and consequently eggs could be destroyed. Observe nesting cranes only from a distance.

SANDHILL CRANE

Photo by Michael Quinton.

GREAT GRAY OWL
(Strix nebulosa)

IDENTIFICATION FEATURES
1. Large, gray or brown-gray, round-headed (earless) owl.
2. Concentric-ringed facial disc.
3. Yellow eyes, yellow beak.
4. Call: a series of deep WHOOOs, successively lower in pitch.
5. Sexes similar.

POSSIBLE IDENTIFICATION CONFUSION
Great Horned Owl: widely spaced ear tufts; gray-black beak; facial disc lacks concentric rings.

MONTHLY OCCURRENCE

J	F	M	A	M	J	J	A	S	O	N	D

Best months for observation: June, July, and August.

LIFE ZONES

	Foothills	Montane	Subalpine	Alpine
Summer		▬▬▬▬▬▬▬▬		
Winter		▬▬▬▬▬▬▬▬		

HABITAT
Open and forested: open meadows, forest clearings, mature stands of conifers.

BEST OBSERVATION POINTS
18   Cascade Meadows
33   Floating Island Lake

BEST GENERAL AREA
Canyon Junction, Tower-Roosevelt

CHANCES OF FINDING THE
GREAT GRAY OWL IN YELLOWSTONE
Hard to see, hard to hear. Result: difficult chance.

POPULATION STATUS
Variable (minor population fluctuations from year to year).

OVERALL ABUNDANCE
U   Uncommon. Less than one hundred pairs of Great Gray Owls are believed to nest in Yellowstone. Because of the secretive habits of this species it is designated as uncommon.

NESTS AND NESTING
Nesting evidence is well established. The Great Gray Owl's nest is a large hollowed cavity in a tree, usually a severed trunk of a tree; the owl may also use an abandoned raptor's nest. Great Gray Owls are laying eggs as early as late April, when there is still an ample amount of snow on the ground. They lay two to five eggs, commonly three. Young owls fledge any time from mid-June to early August.

FOODS AND FEEDING

The principal prey of the Great Gray Owl is the pocket gopher, though it does take hares, pine squirrels, mice, and small birds in the winter. The Great Gray Owl hunts from an elevated perch.

MOVEMENTS AND WINTERING

Great Gray Owls are usually observed singly or in pairs. Some pairs remain in Yellowstone year round, while others migrate to lower elevations in the winter, where prey is more plentiful.

INTERESTING FACTS

The name for the genus *Strix* is believed to have originated from the Greek word *strigx*, derived from *strido*, which means "to utter shrill, harsh sounds." *Nebulosa* is Latin for "cloudy," which describes the gray plumage, and the personality, of this owl. The Great Gray Owl—so called because of its obvious color and size—appears to be larger than it actually is. This owl actually ranks third in overall measurements among North American owls. It is the longest, and it has the longest tail, but that is as far as it goes. The Snowy Owl and the Great Horned Owl surpass it in weight, wing span, and egg size. The Great Gray Owl is one of Yellowstone's best kept secrets. It is a secretive, yet tame, owl. A nocturnal hunter, it can also be found hunting during the crepuscular hours of the day.

Photo by Michael Quinton.

WILLIAMSON'S SAPSUCKER
(Sphyrapicus thyroideus)

IDENTIFICATION FEATURES
1. Sexes *very* different:
   Male: black upperparts and breast; two white stripes on
   black head; red throat; white wing patch; bright yellow
   belly.
   Female: dark brown and white barring on back, wings,
   and sides; brown head; yellow belly.
2. Both sexes have white rump.
3. Slightly smaller than an American Robin.

POSSIBLE IDENTIFICATION CONFUSION
   Red-naped Sapsucker, formerly considered a race of the

Yellow-bellied Sapsucker: red crown and red on back of neck.

MONTHLY OCCURRENCE

J	F	M	A	M	J	J	A	S	O	N	D

Best months for observation: May, June, and July.

LIFE ZONES

Foothills	Montane	Subalpine	Alpine

HABITAT
Open to forested areas: mature Douglas-fir, Douglas fir-aspen, or lodgepole pine forests; aspen combined with open meadows.

BEST OBSERVATION POINTS
23 Tower Fall
35 Blacktail Plateau Drive

BEST GENERAL AREA
Tower-Roosevelt
Mammoth

CHANCES OF FINDING THE
WILLIAMSON'S SAPSUCKER IN YELLOWSTONE
Hard to see, easy to hear. Result: moderate chance.

POPULATION STATUS
Variable (minor population fluctuations from year to year).

OVERALL ABUNDANCE
U Uncommon. Yellowstone's Williamson's Sapsucker population is believed to be less than four hundred nesting pairs. Because of the timid nature of this species, it is regarded as uncommon.

NESTS AND NESTING
Nesting evidence is well established. The nest consists of an excavated cavity in a tree, usually a dead aspen or fir. Williamson's Sapsuckers are first found incubating in these cavities in early to mid-June, around the time elk

calves are born. They lay three to seven eggs, usually five or six. Young sapsuckers fledge in mid- to late July, usually about the time mosquitoes are less abundant.

FOODS AND FEEDING

The food of the Williamson's Sapsucker is primarily insects. The sapsucker is unique in its ability to obtain a rich diet of plant and animal matter from one feeding site. They drill evenly-spaced holes in live trees, and the sap that oozes out is a good food source itself and, most importantly, attracts and entraps insects and ants. Williamson's Sapsuckers also capture insects on the bark of trees and out of the air.

MOVEMENTS AND WINTERING

Williamson's Sapsuckers are extremely timid and are observed most often singly, least often in pairs. Little is known of their movements. They winter in the extreme southern United States and northern Mexico.

INTERESTING FACTS

Sphyrapicus is the genus for sapsuckers; *thyroideus* refers to the red shield-shaped throat patch of the male. Plumages are so different between sexes that for years they were believed to be separate species. The first specimen, a female, was collected in 1852. Robert Williamson was responsible for the railroad survey party in which the first male specimen was collected in 1855. Finally, in 1875, Henry Henshaw discovered that the two supposed species were in fact only the male and female of one species. Williamson's Sapsuckers are found exclusively in North America and take their name from their unique method of boring rows of holes in trees, from which sap drains.

WILLIAMSON'S SAPSUCKER

Photo by Terry McEneaney.

GRAY JAY
(Perisoreus canadensis)

IDENTIFICATION FEATURES
1. Gray body; black feet and bill; white forehead and crown.
2. Long tail; medium bill; no crest.
3. Flight: characteristically flap and glide.
4. Slightly larger than an American Robin.
5. Sexes similar.

POSSIBLE IDENTIFICATION CONFUSION
Clark's Nutcracker: long pointed bill, black wings, white on tail, and white wing patches, visible in flight.

Loggerhead Shrike and Northern Shrike: strongly hooked bills, black masks.

MONTHLY OCCURRENCE

J	F	M	A	M	J	J	A	S	O	N	D

Best months for observation: July, August, and September.

LIFE ZONES

Foothills	Montane	Subalpine	Alpine

HABITAT
Forested areas: coniferous forests, particularly lodgepole pine; commonly found around picnic areas and campgrounds.

BEST OBSERVATION POINTS
14   Yellowstone River
69   Bridge Bay

BEST GENERAL AREA
Bridge Bay

CHANCES OF FINDING THE GRAY JAY IN YELLOWSTONE
Easy to see, easy to hear. Result: excellent chance.

POPULATION STATUS
Variable (minor population fluctuations from year to year).

OVERALL ABUNDANCE
C   Common. Hundreds of Gray Jays reside in Yellowstone throughout the year.

NESTS AND NESTING
Nesting evidence is well established. Nest of small sticks and twigs, often lined with pine needles and grasses, is located on a branch in a tree, usually a conifer. Gray Jays build their nests in late March to mid-April, when there is still snow on the ground. They lay two to five eggs, usually three or four. Young jays fledge from the nest in late April

to mid-May, when patches of bare ground first appear in a landscape covered with snow.

FOODS AND FEEDING
The Gray Jay frequents campgrounds and picnic areas located in coniferous forests and key in on food on or near picnic tables. Besides scavenging food from humans, it has the ability to feed on a wide variety of food items, including insects, nuts, eggs, and even small nestling birds. During stressful periods, the jay returns to areas of stored food, or caches. In the winter it will occasionally feed on carrion.

MOVEMENTS AND WINTERING
Gray Jays are often found in pairs or small flocks. They reside in Yellowstone throughout the year. In the winter they move to forested areas at slightly lower elevations, in search of food.

INTERESTING FACTS
Perisoreus means "food storer," and *canadensis* means Canada. This gray bird was previously known as the Canada Jay where it was first described. It is known by a variety of other common names. The one most commonly applied is "whiskey jack," a name used by hunters and trappers of the north woods. Whiskey jack had nothing to do with hard liquor; it was derived from the Indian name wis-ka-tjon, which was later anglicized to whiskey john and then to whiskey jack. Today the Gray Jay is also referred to as the "camp robber." It is extremely tame and unafraid of humans. It can be extremely quiet or very noisy, and it has the ability to produce a wide variety of calls and whistles. It is an excellent imitator of the calls of other birds, particularly those of the Red-tailed Hawk and the Northern Pygmy-Owl.

Photo by Terry McEneaney.

CLARK'S NUTCRACKER
(Nucifraga columbiana)

IDENTIFICATION FEATURES
1. Gray body; black wings with white patches.
2. Tail has black central and white outer feathers, very conspicuous in flight.
3. Long, fairly heavy, black, pointed bill.
4. Call: a loud, croaking KRA-A-A-A.
5. Larger than an American Robin.
6. Sexes similar.

POSSIBLE IDENTIFICATION CONFUSION
Gray Jay, Loggerhead Shrike, Northern Shrike: smaller; shorter bills; longer tails.
Pinyon Jay: similar shape but smaller; all blue.

MONTHLY OCCURRENCE

J	F	M	A	M	J	J	A	S	O	N	D

Best months for observation: June, July, and August.

CLARK'S NUTCRACKER

LIFE ZONES

	Foothills	Montane	Subalpine	Alpine
Summer		———————————————		
Winter	———————————————			

HABITAT
Open and forested areas: found in a variety of habitats, but prefers extensive stands of conifers.

BEST OBSERVATION POINTS
20   Dunraven Pass
40   Upper Terrace Drive

BEST GENERAL AREA
Mammoth,
    Mount Washburn

CHANCES OF FINDING THE CLARK'S
NUTCRACKER IN YELLOWSTONE
Easy to see, easy to hear. Result: excellent chance.

POPULATION STATUS
Highly variable (major population fluctuations from year to year).

OVERALL ABUNDANCE
A   Abundant. Hundreds of Clark's Nutcrackers reside in Yellowstone throughout the year—they are often encountered on a visit to Yellowstone. Population fluctuations are often tied to fluctuations in the production of pine seeds from year to year.

NESTS AND NESTING
Nesting evidence is well established. The nest, a mass of small sticks or twigs lined with strips of bark and grasses, is usually located on a branch in a conifer. Clark's Nutcrackers nest earlier than any other bird in Yellowstone— late February to late March, when there is still a great amount of snow on the ground. They lay two to six eggs, often four. Young nutcrackers fledge in mid-April to early May, around the time bison calves are born.

FOODS AND FEEDING
The diet of the nutcracker is primarily pine seeds, but it has the ability to feed on a wide variety of food items, ranging from insects and bird eggs in the summer to even car-

rion in the winter. Nutcrackers have a habit of storing food in caches, and they have an incredible memory that allows them to find stored seeds under several feet of snow.

MOVEMENTS AND WINTERING
Nutcrackers are normally found in loose flocks except during the nesting season, when they are found in pairs. They reside in Yellowstone throughout the year. Clark's Nutcrackers are noted for their nomadic and erratic wanderings in search of food. In the fall and winter it is not unusual to find some nutcrackers at lower elevations, while others manage to survive at higher elevations throughout the year.

INTERESTING FACTS
Nucifraga means "nut breaker," *columbiana* refers to the Columbia River of the northwest United States. This bird was first discovered during the Lewis and Clark Expedition of 1805 and was named in honor of Captain William Clark, who mentioned it in his field journal as a "new species of woodpecker." Although for many years it was thought to possess characteristics of both crow and woodpecker, it is indeed a nutcracker, so-called because of the way it extracts nuts from pine cones. They play a key role in the distribution of whitebark pine and limber pine in Yellowstone. The primary propagation method for Whitebark Pine appears to be seedlings sprouting from nutcracker caches. Some individuals have been known to cache thousands of nuts, and distribute them up to several miles from a source tree.

CLARK'S NUTCRACKER

Photo by Karen McEneaney.

COMMON RAVEN
(Corvus corax)

IDENTIFICATION FEATURES
1. Large, all black bird with stout bill.
2. Wedge-shaped tail, usually obvious in flight.
3. Soars more often than the crow.
4. Call is a low-pitched, drawn out CRA-A-A-K.
5. Slightly larger than a Mallard.
6. Sexes similar.

POSSIBLE IDENTIFICATION CONFUSION
American Crow: found at lower elevations; smaller, with smaller head and bill; fan-shaped tail; call is a nasal CA-A-W.

MONTHLY OCCURRENCE

J	F	M	A	M	J	J	A	S	O	N	D

Best months for observation: June, July, and August.

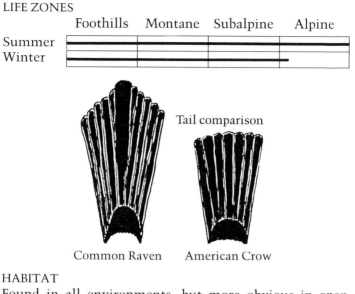

LIFE ZONES

	Foothills	Montane	Subalpine	Alpine
Summer				
Winter				

Tail comparison

Common Raven   American Crow

HABITAT
Found in all environments, but more obvious in open areas.

BEST OBSERVATION POINTS
16   Artist Point
62   Old Faithful

BEST GENERAL AREA
Fishing Bridge
Grand Canyon
   of the Yellowstone

CHANCES OF FINDING THE
COMMON RAVEN IN YELLOWSTONE
Easy to see, easy to hear. Result: excellent chance.

POPULATION STATUS
Increasing.

OVERALL ABUNDANCE
A   Abundant. Hundreds of Common Ravens reside in Yellowstone throughout the year.

NESTS AND NESTING
Nesting evidence is well established. Common Ravens often build large stick nests on cliffs or in trees, beginning usually in late March to mid-April, about the time grizzly bears are emerging from their winter dens. Ravens lay four

to seven eggs, commonly five or six. Young ravens fledge from the nest in late June to mid-July, at the time of year when coyote pups are about half the size of adults.

FOODS AND FEEDING
The raven is omnivorous, meaning that it feeds on both plants and animals. Ecologically, the raven can be classified as a "raptor" because of its rapacious nature at times of obtaining carnivorous prey, although it is not a true bird of prey in the classical sense. Ravens in Yellowstone are often observed chasing other raptors or following mammalian predators to a potential food source. Another adaptation is its ability to find food in the middle of winter—they are often found in close proximity to ungulate herds, where they feed on carrion.

MOVEMENTS AND WINTERING
Common Ravens are found in pairs, but more often in flocks. They are found in Yellowstone in every conceivable habitat throughout the year. Some ravens often move to lower elevations in the winter due to the scarcity of food at higher elevations.

INTERESTING FACTS
Corvus is a genus of the Corvid family that includes crows and ravens, and *corax* means "a croaker." The word raven, which refers to a large black bird with a loud hoarse call and noted for its plundering or rapacious habits, is derived from the old English word *hraefn*, which supposedly describes the cry of the bird. Ravens are perhaps the most successful of all the bird species that inhabit Yellowstone. Its success lies in its ability to adapt to humans, to live in a hostile environment, to eat a wide variety of food items, and to live in a wide variety of habitats. The raven is considered by many native cultures as a hero and a good omen.

Photo by Michael Quinton.

MOUNTAIN CHICKADEE
(Parus gambeli)

IDENTIFICATION FEATURES
1. Tiny gray bird with black cap, eyestripe, and bib.
2. White eyebrow and cheek.
3. Call: hoarse CHICK-A-DEE-DEE-DEE.
   Song: clear, sweet, whistled three or four notes.
4. Smaller than a House sparrow.
5. Sexes similar.

POSSIBLE IDENTIFICATION CONFUSION
Black-capped Chickadee: black cap extends below the eye.

Black-capped Chickadee

Mountain Chickadee

MONTHLY OCCURRENCE

J	F	M	A	M	J	J	A	S	O	N	D

Best months for observation: April, May, and June.

LIFE ZONES

Foothills	Montane	Subalpine	Alpine

HABITAT
Forested areas: prefers coniferous forests.

BEST OBSERVATION POINTS
   7   Fishing Bridge Museum
35   Blacktail Plateau Drive

BEST GENERAL AREA
Tower Fall, Dunraven Pass

CHANCES OF FINDING THE
MOUNTAIN CHICKADEE IN YELLOWSTONE
Easy to see, easy to hear. Result: excellent chance.

POPULATION STATUS
Variable (minor population fluctuations from year to year).

OVERALL ABUNDANCE
A   Abundant. Thousands of Mountain Chickadees reside
in Yellowstone throughout the year.

NESTS AND NESTING

Nesting evidence is well established. Chickadees nest in small cavities in trees, lined with grasses, mosses, fur, and feathers. They lay six to twelve eggs, normally nine, from early to late June, approximately the time moose calves are born. Young chickadees fledge from the nest in late June to early July, around the time young ravens are trying out their acrobatic skills.

FOODS AND FEEDING

The food of the Mountain Chickadee is a variety of small seeds and insects. This bird flies from tree to tree, actively calling as it collects food from the limbs and branches of each tree.

MOVEMENTS AND WINTERING

Mountain Chickadees are often found in pairs or in small flocks. They are found more commonly in mountainous country at higher elevations. They reside in Yellowstone throughout the year. In the winter their numbers are lower and they often move to slightly lower elevations in search of food.

INTERESTING FACTS

The genus *Parus* is derived from the family Paridae, which includes chickadees, titmice, and related species. The parids are small, round, plump birds with small, thin bills. The species *gambeli* refers to Dr. William Gambel, one of the leading field ornithologists in the mid-1800s. The name chickadee is derived from the bird's call. Mountain Chickadees are more commonly found in conifers, while Black-capped Chickadees inhabit mixed or deciduous forests, usually at lower altitudes in Yellowstone. They are both extremely tame and unafraid of humans.

National Park Service

AMERICAN DIPPER
(Cinclus mexicanus)

IDENTIFICATION FEATURES
1. Plump, slate gray bird; short tail.
2. Typical bobbing action as it stands on rocks, logs, etc.
3. Almost always associated with rushing streams.
4. Direct flight over stream with rapid wing-beats.
5. Somewhat smaller than an American robin.
6. Sexes similar.

POSSIBLE IDENTIFICATION CONFUSION
One of a kind—should not be confused with any other species.

MONTHLY OCCURRENCE

J	F	M	A	M	J	J	A	S	O	N	D

Best months for observation: May, June, and December.

LIFE ZONES

	Foothills	Montane	Subalpine	Alpine
Summer		▬▬▬▬	▬▬▬▬	
Winter	▬▬▬▬	▬▬▬▬	▬▬▬	

HABITAT
Water: rushing mountain streams and creeks.

BEST OBSERVATION POINTS
53 Gibbon River
58 Firehole Canyon Drive

BEST GENERAL AREA
Firehole Canyon
Gardner River

CHANCES OF FINDING THE
AMERICAN DIPPER IN YELLOWSTONE
Easy to see, easy to hear. Result: excellent chance.

POPULATION STATUS
Variable (minor population fluctuations from year to year).

OVERALL ABUNDANCE
C Common. Hundreds of dippers are found in Yellowstone throughout the year.

NESTS AND NESTING
Nesting evidence is well established. Nest consists of a dome-shaped mass of mosses, often precariously hanging over rushing water either on the side of a rock, on a cliff, or sometimes even underneath a bridge. American Dippers are building their nests around mid-May to early June, before high spring runoff occurs. They lay three to six eggs, commonly four or five. Young dippers fledge in late June to mid-July, which is about the time spring runoff recedes. During favorable circumstances some dipper pairs produce two broods in a single season.

FOODS AND FEEDING
American Dippers feed mainly on water insects. Fly fishermen in the West watch this bird very closely, for the dipper is skilled at catching insects and insect larvae. Experienced fly fishermen have learned to duplicate the insect larvae that the dipper feeds on, hoping to increase their chances of catching a trout. The typical behavior of a dipper con-

sists of bobbing up and down on the rocks in the middle of a creek or river. They are expert swimmers and can grub for insects by walking underwater, which they accomplish by grabbing onto rocks with their feet.

MOVEMENTS AND WINTERING
American Dippers are found singly or in pairs. They are found in Yellowstone throughout the year. In the winter, some dippers are forced to move to lower elevations in search of open water and available food. The lower end of the Gardner River is an excellent place to observe high concentrations of American Dippers in the winter.

INTERESTING FACTS
The genus *Cinclus* is derived from the family Cinclidae, the dipper family; *mexicanus* means Mexico. The range of the American Dipper is restricted to the mountains of western North America, from Panama to Alaska. The name dipper refers to this bird's unique bobbing or dipping behavior when it perches on a rock or log in a stream. American Dippers are well adapted to their water environment. They possess an extremely large preen, or oil, gland, keeping their feathers waterproof. They also have a moveable flap covering the nostrils, which keeps water out when they dive, and a nictitating membrane over the eyes, which keeps them clear of water droplets. In Britain, dippers are also commonly called "water ousels."

Photo by Michael Quinton.

MOUNTAIN BLUEBIRD
(Sialia curricoides)

IDENTIFICATION FEATURES
1. Male: deep sky-blue above and pale blue below.
2. Female: gray-brown bird with blue wash in wings and tail.
3. Slightly smaller than an American robin.

POSSIBLE IDENTIFICATION CONFUSION
Townsend's Solitaire: lacks blue wings; has a larger tail than the female bluebird.
Pinyon Jay: longer, pointed bill; larger size; plumage more gray-blue than that of the male bluebird.

MONTHLY OCCURRENCE

J	F	M	A	M	J	J	A	S	O	N	D
									•	•	

Best months for observation: April, May, and June.

LIFE ZONES

Foothills	Montane	Subalpine	Alpine

HABITAT
Open areas: sagebrush-grassland, geyser basins, mountain meadows, up to timberline; bordering dead snags and/or scattered conifers.

BEST OBSERVATION POINTS
26   Roosevelt Lodge
40   Upper Terrace Drive

BEST GENERAL AREA
Mammoth, Tower-Roosevelt, Norris

CHANCES OF FINDING THE MOUNTAIN BLUEBIRD IN YELLOWSTONE
Easy to see, easy to hear. Result: excellent chance.

POPULATION STATUS
Variable (minor population fluctuations from year to year).

OVERALL ABUNDANCE
C   Common. Hundreds of Mountain Bluebirds nest in Yellowstone.

NEST AND NESTING
Nesting evidence is well established. Nest consists of a small cavity, often lined with grasses and weeds, usually in a tree but occasionally in a building. Nest building occurs in late May, well before the peak of the insect hatch. Mountain Bluebirds lay four to eight eggs, often five or six. Young bluebirds fledge any time from mid-June to late July, depending on the elevation and whether one or two broods fledge in any particular year.

FOODS AND FEEDING
Mountain Bluebirds feed almost exclusively on insects, although berries are part of their diet in the fall and winter. In Yellowstone they are conspicuously found on dead snags or branches, from which they drop down to the ground for

MOUNTAIN BLUEBIRD   103 insects. They can also catch insects in flight, and they are experts at hovering.

MOVEMENTS AND WINTERING
Mountain Bluebirds are often found in pairs, family groups, or small flocks. They arrive when there is still much snow on the ground—along with American Robins, they are usually the first of the migrant birds to arrive in Yellowstone in the spring. In the winter, Mountain Bluebirds migrate out of the Park to the southwestern United States and northern Mexico.

INTERESTING FACTS
Sialia, the genus for bluebird, supposedly refers to its hissing or off-tune warble. *Currucoides* purportedly relates to the warbler-like appearance of the Mountain Bluebird. The Mountain Bluebird calls either in flight or from a perch. It is well-named, for it frequents mountainous or foothill country. In Yellowstone the Mountain Bluebird is the true harbinger of spring.

MOUNTAIN BLUEBIRD

Photo by Terry McEneaney.

DARK-EYED JUNCO
(Junco hyemalis)

IDENTIFICATION FEATURES
1. Similar size and shape as a House Sparrow.
2. Gray or brown upper parts and breast, in varying combinations and shades according to race (see field guides).
3. Gray, brown, or pinkish sides.
4. Small pink bill, white belly, prominent white outer tail feathers.

POSSIBLE IDENTIFICATION CONFUSION
Vesper Sparrow and Lark Sparrow: streaked backs; found in more open habitats; have white in tails.

MONTHLY OCCURRENCE

J	F	M	A	M	J	J	A	S	O	N	D
•	•										•

Best months for observation: June, July, and September.

LIFE ZONES

Foothills	Montane	Subalpine	Alpine

HABITAT
Forested areas: forest openings, forest edge; aspen-conifer or coniferous forests with grass understory.

BEST OBSERVATION POINTS
23 Tower Fall
52 Gibbon Falls Picnic Area

BEST GENERAL AREAS
Norris, Tower-Roosevelt, Mammoth

CHANCES OF FINDING THE DARK-EYED JUNCO IN YELLOWSTONE
Easy to see, easy to hear. Result: excellent chance.

POPULATION STATUS
Variable (minor population fluctuations from year to year).

OVERALL ABUNDANCE
A Abundant. The Dark-eyed Junco is probably the most abundant bird in Yellowstone. Each year thousands nest in the Park.

NESTS AND NESTING
Nesting evidence is well established. Dark-eyed Juncos nest on the ground, usually in the grass understory of a forest, and the nest consists almost entirely of grasses. They build their nests in June, after the winter snows have disappeared from the forest understory. They lay three to five eggs, often four. Young juncos fledge in July, by the time most plants have flowered and seeds are readily available.

FOODS AND FEEDING
Dark-eyed Juncos forage on the ground, where they pick up seeds and sometimes insects. Unlike sparrows, they do not scratch the ground for food, but rather hop around, picking up food off the surface.

MOVEMENTS AND WINTERING
Only during the breeding season are juncos paired—most

of the time they are found in flocks. Juncos, because of their restrictive feeding habits, are forced to winter in the southern United States. They leave late in the fall, after the food resources are exhausted, and return in late winter and early spring, when patches of bare ground are visible at lower elevations. Juncos are found periodically in the Mammoth area in the winter, but these observations are rare.

INTERESTING FACTS

Junco is the genus for these small, sparrow-like birds, and *hyemalis* means "winter." Juncos are often referred to as snowbirds, because when they migrate to their wintering areas their arrival often predicts the coming of winter. Juncos also return to Yellowstone in the spring, when there is still snow on the ground. During these cold, stressful periods, juncos often enter small caves and cisterns in geyser and hot spring areas, trying to keep warm, and become victims of gas asphyxiation.

The Oregon Junco and the Slate-colored Junco were once considered separate species, but because these birds have been found to hybridize, they are today considered to be members of the same species and are combined under the name Dark-eyed Junco (*Junco hyemalis*). There are a number of subspecies or races of the Dark-eyed Junco in North America. The Pink-sided Junco (*J. h. mearnsi*) nests in Yellowstone and is the subspecies you are most likely to encounter. This junco has a rather pale gray head with black lores and broad pink sides and flanks. Occasionally Slate-colored Juncos (*J. h. hyemalis*) and Montana Oregon Juncos (*J. h. montanus*) show up during migration, and on rare occasions are found wintering in Yellowstone.

Photo by Terry McEneaney

ROSY FINCH
(Leucosticte arctoa)

IDENTIFICATION FEATURES
1. Similar size and shape as a House Sparrow.
2. Stocky little bird with brown or black body.
3. Light pink or rosy rump, belly, and wash on wings.
4. Gray crown, black forehead.
5. See field guide for plumage variation of races.
6. Female similar but duller color than male.

POSSIBLE IDENTIFICATION CONFUSION
Cassin's Finch: red or pink breast.
Common Redpoll: red cap, black chin, white or pink breast.

MONTHLY OCCURRENCE

J	F	M	A	M	J	J	A	S	O	N	D

Best months for observation: February, March, June, and July.

ROSY FINCH

LIFE ZONES

	Foothills	Montane	Subalpine	Alpine
Summer				━━━━━
Winter	━━━━━			━━━━━

HABITAT
Open areas: in summer, grassy, rocky areas of the alpine; in winter, grassland or meadow areas, with higher incidence of occurrence at lower elevations.

BEST OBSERVATION POINTS
21   Mount Washburn (summer)
38   Mammoth Campground
      (winter)

BEST GENERAL AREA
Mount Washburn

CHANCES OF FINDING THE
ROSY FINCH IN YELLOWSTONE
Easy to see, hard to hear. Result: moderate chance.

POPULATION STATUS
Variable (minor population fluctuations from year to year).

OVERALL ABUNDANCE
U   Uncommon. Hundreds of Rosy Finches are found in Yellowstone throughout the year, but due to the difficult access of its habitat in summer and its nomadic behavior in winter, it is regarded as uncommon.

NESTS AND NESTING
Nesting evidence is well established. The nest of a Rosy Finch consists of dried grasses or mosses in cliff ledges, rock crevices, or sheltered rocks. They are nest building any time from early to late June, when there are still snow-fields on the mountain summits, and they lay four to five eggs. The young fledge from mid-July to late August, during the height of the thunderstorm season.

FOODS AND FEEDING
Rosy Finches are found almost exclusively on the ground, where they eat primarily seeds, although insects have been documented. In the early summer they are frequently seen feeding in open areas on the edge of retreating snowbanks.

In the summer they frequent the rocky alpine areas of mountain summits, whereas in winter they are found in open areas at lower elevations, in search of food.

MOVEMENTS AND WINTERING

Rosy Finches reside in Yellowstone throughout the year. In the summer they are paired or in small family groups and use almost exclusively the alpine environment. In the fall and winter they gather in large flocks and, due to food shortages, are forced to move to lower elevations in and outside of Yellowstone. They are extremely active and constantly on the move.

Races of Rosy Finches found in Yellowstone, from left to right: Black; Gray-crowned; Hepburn's.

Rosy Finch bill color variation: winter (left) and summer (right)

INTERESTING FACTS

Leucosticte means "white line," and *arctoa* means "arctic." This scientific name refers to the close association of Rosy Finches to the snowline or snowfields. The common name refers to the rosy-pink coloration of its plumage. It is not unusual to find Rosy Finches roosting in cliff swallow nests in the winter.

There are three races or subspecies of Rosy Finch found in Yellowstone: The Black Rosy Finch (*L. a. atrata*) is the subspecies most often encountered in the summer. In the winter, all three races can be found—the Gray-crowned Rosy Finch (*L. a. tephrocotis*) and the Black Rosy Finch are the most common, while the Hepburn's Rosy Finch (*L. a. littoralis*), occurs in very limited numbers.

ROSY FINCH

4

TRAVELING THE ROADS OF YELLOWSTONE—A JOURNEY THROUGH BIRD HABITATS

ROADS, TO SOME PEOPLE, MAY SEEM FOREIGN and unnatural, but they are undeniably a part of the Yellowstone ecosystem and the Yellowstone experience. Roads are habitats for some birds. Common Ravens and raptors feed on road-killed mammals on road surfaces and in banks and ditches. Other man-made structures such as signs, telephone poles, wires, buildings, and bridges provide perches or nest sites for birds–some hawks and owls use telephone poles as vantage points from which to hunt for prey. Holes in buildings create nest sites for European Starlings, American Kestrels, and Mountain Bluebirds. Cliff Swallows and American Dippers nest under certain bridges in Yellowstone. Humans, while destroying habitat in some places, have in other cases created bird habitat in Yellowstone.

As you drive through Yellowstone, picture the roads cutting across different micro-habitats, each harboring different birds. Each road in Yellowstone is a different sampling of habitats. Whenever you drive a road—whether here in Yellowstone or anywhere else—try to think of the road as a "transect" through different habitats, and try to remember what species of birds you have seen in those habitats at different seasons. As you travel the roads of Yellowstone, get in the habit of identifying bird habitats and thinking of what species to expect there. Bird-finding will then come more easily for you.

The following section tells you what to expect while traveling the roads of Yellowstone. The descriptions will

Fig. 11. Brown-headed Cowbirds on the back of a bison. Author photo.

give you a general idea of the relief of the landscape, the diversity of habitat found along each road, and the types of birds to expect. This gives you a chance to decide which roads to choose on your visit to the Park. (Note: Since the greatest diversity of birds occurs in the summer, these generalizations about birds apply primarily to the summer months.)

GARDINER TO MAMMOTH ROAD

Road Distance: 5 Miles/8Kilometers

Road Map

Road Location in Yellowstone

```
                                    →
                                    N
    45th Parallel
      Bridge  - - - - - .
Mammoth,    •  \39        • Gardiner,
Wyoming      •              Montana
6239'       38              5314'
```

Road Relief Cross Section

```
Life Zone   Mammoth,Wyo.
   Montane   6239'  45th Parallel Bridge
- - - - -                Gardiner, Montana
 Foothills              5314'
```

On the drive from Gardiner, Montana, up to Mammoth, Wyoming, you will pass through a diversity of habitats and through two distinct life zones, the foothills zone and the montane zone. The change from one zone to another is not that apparent, but it occurs in the vicinity of the 45th Parallel Bridge ③⑨.

On your way from Gardiner to Mammoth look for Western Meadowlarks, Vesper Sparrows, Cliff Swallows, and American Kestrels. Along the fast-flowing Gardner River look for American Dippers and Belted Kingfishers. At the 45th Parallel Bridge, look for Lazuli Buntings, Chipping Sparrows, Cliff Swallows and Barn Swallows. As the road gets steeper, look for Red-tailed Hawks and Golden Eagles circle-soaring. Or better yet, you may get lucky and see a Prairie Falcon stoop at a ground squirrel. As you approach Mammoth campground ③⑧ , look in the conifers for Red-breasted Nuthatches, Mountain Chickadees, Mountain Bluebirds, Three-toed Woodpeckers, Hairy Woodpeckers, Clark's Nutcrackers, Pine Siskins, and Cassin's Finches. Black-billed Magpies are easily found in the Mammoth Area.

As a possible side trip, try traveling the Stevens Creek Road, which is a dirt road that begins at the Roosevelt Arch in Gardiner, Montana and heads northwest through the foothills zone. This is an excellent road for observing Sage Thrashers and Horned Larks.

MAMMOTH TO NORRIS ROAD

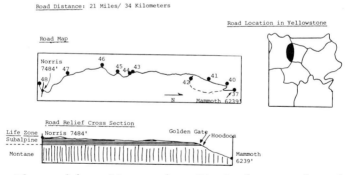

The road from Mammoth to Norris also cuts through many habitats and through two distinct life zones, the montane zone and the subalpine zone. The change from one zone to another is not obvious but occurs in the vicinity of a rock rubble area called the Hoodoos ④⑴ and a gold-colored rock face appropriately called Golden Gate.

At lower elevations, especially near the Mammoth Museum-Albright Visitor Center ㊲ , look or listen for Cassin's Finches, Red-naped Sapsuckers, Yellow Warblers, and Warbling Vireos. At the hot springs and terraces around Mammoth look for a Mountain Bluebird perched on a dead branch of a conifer. The wooded section above the Upper Terrace ㊵ is perhaps the best place in Yellowstone to find the elusive Townsend's Solitaire. As you gain elevation on the road, stop at the Hoodoos and look and listen for Rock Wrens and Clark's Nutcrackers. When you reach the subalpine zone above Golden Gate, look for Red-tailed Hawks and Swainson's Hawks in the open meadows. If you are extremely lucky, you may get the opportunity to hear the primitive calls of Sandhill Cranes. For a side tour, take the Bunsen Peak road ㊷ ; this one-way dirt road is excellent for observing Tree Swallows, Hairy Woodpeckers, Downy Woodpeckers, Green-tailed Towhees, Red-naped Sapsuckers, and, near Osprey Falls look for White-throated Swifts, Violet-green Swallows, and Prairie Falcons. Resuming the trip again along the Mammoth to Norris road, continue south along a flat sagebrush area known as Swan Lake Flats. In the sagebrush, look and listen for Vesper Sparrows, Brewer's Sparrows, and Savannah Sparrows. As you continue, especially in the thick willow stands along Obsidian Creek ㊸ , look for Wilson's Warblers, Song Sparrows, White-crowned Sparrows, and Lincoln Sparrows. At Apollinaris Spring ㊹ , look for Yellow-rumped Warbler's, Ruby-crowned Kinglets, and Hermit Thrushes. Common Ravens are found almost anywhere along this road. At Beaver Lake near Obsidian Cliff ㊺ , look and listen for Soras and Common Snipes. At the site of the old forest fire burn ㊻ look for Olive-sided Flycatchers, Three-toed Woodpeckers, and Dark-eyed Juncos; and at Twin Lakes ㊼ look for Barrow's Goldeneyes.

MADISON TO NORRIS ROAD

Although this road lies entirely within the subalpine zone, it still crosses a diversity of habitats: forests, open meadows, rivers, hot springs, rapids, and waterfalls.

At Terrace Springs, which is one-half mile north of Madison Junction, look and listen for Mountain Bluebirds, Killdeers, and Red Crossbills. Along the fast flowing Gib-

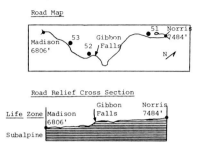

Road Location in Yellowstone

bon River ⑤₃ , keep an eye open for American Dippers. At Gibbon Falls ⑤₂ look for Violet-green Swallows and Common Ravens. In the open meadows ⑤₁ look for Savannah Sparrows. And at Norris Geyser Basin ④₈ look for Mountain Bluebirds in the trees and Killdeers on the ground near the thermal features.

WEST YELLOWSTONE TO MADISON ROAD

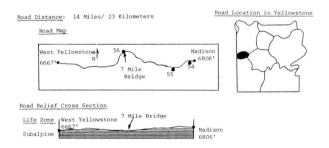

You may want to look around West Yellowstone for a bit before you begin your journey east to Madison. Common Ravens are found right in the middle of town – they can be seen flying, perched in a tree, or eating food out of a garbage dumpster.

The road from West Yellowstone to Madison lies entirely within the subalpine zone and is interesting because it parallels the Madison River. Seven miles east of West Yellowstone is a pullout area next to the river known as Seven Mile Bridge ㊏ . This is perhaps the best place in Yellowstone to observe Trumpeter Swans. Visitors are cautioned not to disturb them – Park rangers monitor the swans hourly and have been known to issue citations for harassing them. Canada Geese and Mallards can also be observed from this road ㊺ . In the open meadows near Madison Junction ㊾ , look for Red-tailed Hawks soaring. Try looking in the vicinity of the Madison campground for Three-toed Woodpeckers. Common Nighthawks can be seen in this area, soaring over open meadows around dusk; listen for their nasal "peent" call or the roaring sound they make with their wings as they dive.

GALLATIN ROAD (GRAYLING CREEK TO CROWN BUTTE)

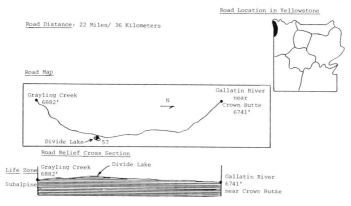

Road Location in Yellowstone

Road Distance: 22 Miles/ 36 Kilometers

Road Map

Grayling Creek
6882'

N

Gallatin River
near
Crown Butte
6741'

Divide Lake 57

Road Relief Cross Section

Life Zone   Grayling Creek   Divide Lake
             6882'

Subalpine

Gallatin River
6741'
near Crown Butte

This road lies entirely within the subalpine zone and is not a very interesting one for birdwatching. As one travels from Grayling Creek north along Highway 191 to Crown Butte, look for American Dippers along the fast moving Grayling Creek. In the conifers around the same area, keep an eye open for Steller's Jays and Swainson's Thrushes. In the willows bordering the streams, look for White-crowned Sparrows, Lincoln Sparrows, Song Sparrows, and Wilson's Warblers. Look for Mallards at Divide Lake ㊼ . Divide Lake is also a good place to observe shorebirds during fall migration. In the open meadows, look for raptors such as Red-tailed Hawks.

BECHLER AREA

There is a small section of road in the remote southwest corner of Yellowstone National Park known as the Bechler area ㊻ . It is an out-of-the-way area and requires a great

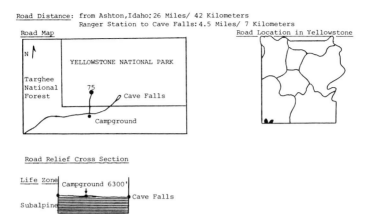

Road Distance: from Ashton,Idaho: 26 Miles/ 42 Kilometers
Ranger Station to Cave Falls: 4.5 Miles/ 7 Kilometers

Road Map — Road Location in Yellowstone

N
YELLOWSTONE NATIONAL PARK
Targhee National Forest
75
Cave Falls
Campground

Road Relief Cross Section

Life Zone
Campground 6300'
Cave Falls
Subalpine

deal of time to get there. From Aston, Idaho, drive northeast on the Cave Falls Road for twenty-six miles. The road is primarily a gravel road. There are less than five miles of road to drive on once you are in the Park. The road lies entirely within the subalpine zone. If you like to hike while watching birds this may be for you, but the mosquitoes and inclement weather at times tend to turn people away.

Because of the diversity of habitats in this area, the birding is quite good. Some of the birds you might see include: American Dippers, Spotted Sandpipers, Hermit Thrushes, American Robins, Sandhill Cranes, Great Gray Owls, Red-naped Sapsuckers, Hairy Woodpeckers, Mountain Chickadees, Black-capped Chickadees, Tree Swallows, Cassin's Finches, Ruby-crowned Kinglets, Yellow Warblers, Yellow-rumped Warblers, Wilson's Warblers, Yellowthroats, and Song Sparrows.

MADISON TO OLD FAITHFUL ROAD

This road lies entirely within the subalpine zone and although the habitats along it are not that diverse, it is still a road worth birding. In the vicinity of Firehole Falls, look for American Dippers along the fast-flowing water of the Firehole River ⑤⑧ . On the slow-flowing sections of the river, you may get lucky and find Great Blue Herons stalking fish along the riverbank. In the wide-open meadows look for Common Ravens and Brown-headed Cowbirds. Brown-headed Cowbirds are quite commonly found as-

ROADS OF YELLOWSTONE 119

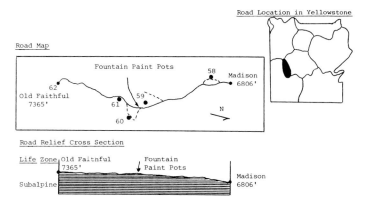

Road Location in Yellowstone

Road Map

Fountain Paint Pots

58
Madison
6806'

62
Old Faithful
7365'

59

61

60

N

Road Relief Cross Section

Life Zone | Old Faithful
7365'

Fountain
Paint Pots

Madison
6806'

Subalpine

sociated with bison in Yellowstone, often perching on the backs of bison to pick at insects and ticks or sometimes just to stay warm. In the Fountain Flats area ⑤⑨ , which is a wide-open meadow, stop and listen for Sandhill Cranes, especially if you are there in the morning or evening, when they are much more vocal. In the geyser basin areas ⑥⓪ , listen for the drilling sound of woodpeckers such as Northern Flickers and Hairy Woodpeckers. The drilling sound can usually be traced to a bird in a dead or dying conifer. Around the geyser basins look for Mountain Bluebirds in dead trees or trees with dead branches. Bluebirds often flycatch for insects from these elevated perches. Soras can usually be heard calling from the sedges of a sediment-filled lake known as Whiskey Flats ⑥① . Killdeers are also commonly found in the geyser basins wading on or near these shallow water thermal areas ⑥②

OLD FAITHFUL TO WEST THUMB ROAD

This road lies entirely within the subalpine zone. It is one of the most heavily-wooded roads in Yellowstone, and one of the most uneventful ones for birdwatching. Mountain Chickadees and Dark-eyed Juncos can be found almost anywhere along this road. The Old Faithful area ⑥② is just an average birding area. Common Ravens, Killdeers, and Northern Flickers are often seen in the vicinity of Old Faithful. Along the road to West Thumb, there are few

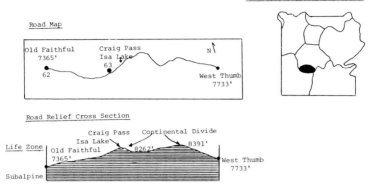

forest openings, and due to the monotypic nature of the forest vegetation there is very little habitat diversity. Barrow's Goldeneyes are often found on a small lake known as Scaup Lake ⑥ , which is situated in the middle of the lodgepole pine forest. A good observer should not be caught napping, however, for one may get a glimpse of Northern Goshawks, Cassin's Finches, Red Crossbills, or Steller's Jays flying across the road. If you do stop at a picnic area along the way you will probably see Gray Jays; these bold and assertive birds are commonly found around picnickers in the summer. In the conifers near West Thumb, Swainson's Thrushes and Hermit Thrushes can often be found.

WEST THUMB TO SOUTH ENTRANCE ROAD

This road, lying entirely within the subalpine zone, runs mainly through forests, with openings at such places as Lewis Lake, Lewis River, and Lewis Canyon. The birding is not overly exciting on this drive through the conifers from West Thumb to the South Entrance, but Grant Village ⑪ is one of the best birding areas in the southern part of the Park. A trip down by the lakefront could reward you with sightings of Spotted Sandpipers, Ospreys, and even Common Mergansers. At Lewis Lake ⑫ look for Barrow's Goldeneyes. In the willows along the Lewis River look for Wilson's Warblers, Lincoln's Sparrows, and White-crowned Sparrows. In the Lewis Canyon area ⑬ look for

ROADS OF YELLOWSTONE   121

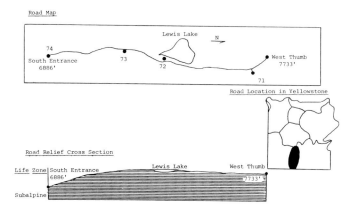

Road Map

Lewis Lake

N

74
South Entrance
6886'

73

72

West Thumb
7733'

71

Road Location in Yellowstone

Road Relief Cross Section

Life Zone | South Entrance
6886'

Lewis Lake

West Thumb
7733'

Subalpine

American Dippers on rocks near the fast-flowing water. Along the canyon rim look for Common Ravens, Violet-green Swallows, and Clark's Nutcrackers. In the forested sections along this road keep your eyes peeled for Red Crossbills. These nomadic wanderers travel these extensive forests in search of pine seeds. Near the South Entrance ⑦④ look for Spotted Sandpipers and Canada Geese along the banks of the Snake River.

WEST THUMB TO FISHING BRIDGE ROAD

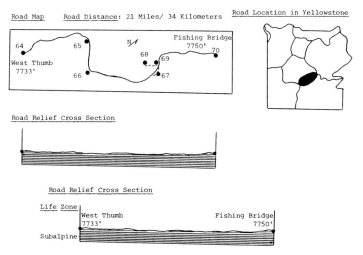

Road Map   Road Distance: 21 Miles/ 34 Kilometers   Road Location in Yellowstone

64   65
West Thumb
7733'

N

Fishing Bridge
7750'   70

68   69

66   67

Road Relief Cross Section

Road Relief Cross Section

Life Zone
West Thumb
7733'

Fishing Bridge
7750'

Subalpine

This relatively flat road, which lies entirely within the Yellowstone caldera and the subalpine zone, is the longest stretch of road that borders Yellowstone Lake. At West Thumb ⑥④ , on Yellowstone Lake, look for California Gulls, Green-winged Teal, and, if you are lucky, Common Loons. Look for Ospreys and Bald Eagles perched in trees along the lakeshore ⑥⑤ ⑥⑥ ⑥⑦ , waiting for the right moment to snatch a surfacing cutthroat trout. Between Pumice Point ⑥⑥ and Gull Point Drive ⑥⑦ you will pass through the most distinctive spruce-fir habitat found near the roads in Yellowstone. In this area look for Brown Creepers, Golden-crowned Kinglets, Ruby-crowned Kinglets, Mountain Chickadees, Red-breasted Nuthatches, Swainson's Thrushes, and Hermit Thrushes. Gull Point Drive ⑥⑦ passes by three unique microenvironments of Yellowstone Lake which include a beach, a lagoon, and a sandspit. Another option to consider is to take the road to Natural Bridge ⑥⑧ – this is a good place to observe Yellow-rumped Warblers. At Bridge Bay ⑥⑨ look for Lesser Scaup, California Gulls, and Ring-billed Gulls. At Lake ⑦⓪ look for Red-breasted Nuthatches and Cassin's Finches in the conifers. If you are lucky, you may spot Great Gray Owls in the open meadows near Lake.

FISHING BRIDGE TO EAST ENTRANCE ROAD

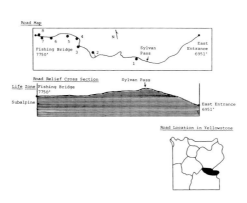

Road Distance: 27 Miles/ 43 Kilometers

Road Map

Fishing Bridge 7750' Sylvan Pass East Entrance 6951'

Road Relief Cross Section Sylvan Pass

Life Zone Fishing Bridge 7750'

Subalpine East Entrance 6951'

Road Location in Yellowstone

The habitat is quite varied along this road, which lies entirely within the subalpine zone. At Fishing Bridge ⑧ look for American White Pelicans trying to snatch up cutthroat trout. Mallards, California Gulls, Ospreys and occasionally Bald Eagles are observed from Fishing Bridge. At Fishing Bridge Museum ⑦ stop and walk around, looking and listening for Ruby-crowned Kinglets and Yellow-rumped Warblers. Some of the rarest and most unusual birds in Yellowstone have been recorded in this general area. At the Pelican Bridge area ⑥ look for Green-winged Teal, Soras, Ospreys, American White Pelicans, and occasionally Northern Harriers. At Indian Lake ⑤ look for Lesser Scaup, and in the moist open meadows look for Savannah Sparrows. Migrating songbirds funnel through this area in the fall, providing one of the best chances for observing Sharp-shinned Hawks and Cooper's Hawks in Yellowstone. At Mary Bay ④ look out on the lake for Common Loons. On the sandy shoreline of Yellowstone Lake look for California Gulls, Ring-billed Gulls, and occasionally Willets and Common Terns. Steamboat Point ③ is a great place to observe Common Loons, especially in June, September, and October. A drive up to Lake Butte overlook ② provides you not only with one of the best views of Yellowstone Lake and the Yellowstone wilderness, but also with a great opportunity to find Blue Grouse and Clark's Nutcrackers. At Sylvan Lake ① look carefully for Barrow's Goldeneyes. From Sylvan Pass to the East Entrance the road passes mainly through high mountain country. Common Ravens and Clark's Nutcrackers are often found here.

CANYON TO FISHING BRIDGE ROAD

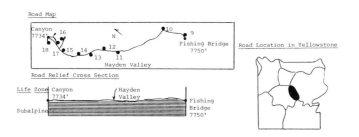

This road lies entirely within the subalpine zone and is one of the most interesting roads for the birdwatcher. At Cascade Meadows ⑱ look for Swainson's Hawks and Common Ravens. At Lookout Point ⑰ look around for Ospreys flying in the canyon, and in the lodgepole pines look for Yellow-rumped Warblers. At Artist Point ⑯ look for Ospreys, Violet-green Swallows and Common Ravens in the canyon. At Chittenden Bridge ⑮ in the spring you may get lucky and see a Harlequin Duck in the rapids of the Yellowstone River. Along the Yellowstone River ⑭ look for Ospreys attempting to catch fish either by hovering or by hunting from an elevated perch. Spotted Sandpipers are often found along the shore of the slow-flowing portions of the river. The Alum Creek pullout ⑬ is an excellent roadside area for birding and is worth a stop. In the open wet meadows of Hayden Valley, near the Grizzly Overlook ⑫ , listen for Sandhill Cranes. In the sagebrush areas look for Vesper Sparrows and Savannah Sparrows. Swainson's Hawks can be found in this same type of habitat. Near Trout Creek ⑪ look for Cliff Swallows and Bank Swallows. Near Mud Volcano, in the open areas, look for Brown-headed Cowbirds near bison herds. In the vicinity of LeHardy Rapids ⑩ , keep an eye open for Gray Jays in the conifers. Along the Yellowstone River look for Buffleheads, Barrow's Goldeneyes, Canada Geese, Mallards, American White Pelicans, and Common Mergansers. In the open meadow close to Fishing Bridge ⑨ look for Swainson's Hawks and Savannah Sparrows.

NORRIS TO CANYON ROAD

Road Distance: 12 Miles/ 19 Kilometers

Road Map

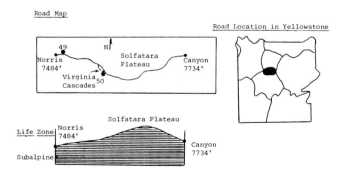

Road Location in Yellowstone

This road, which lies entirely within the subalpine zone, is not very interesting for birdwatching. Near Norris ㊾ listen for Common Snipes in the open wet meadows. At Virginia Cascade Meadows ㊿   look for American Dippers. In the meadow above the actual cascades look in the willows for Wilson's Warblers and Lincoln's Sparrows. Chipping Sparrows can usually be found where the dry meadows and the conifers merge. Between Virginia Cascades and Canyon, you will find an area where trees have been blown down by a storm and another area where there once was a forest fire—try searching here for Three-toed Woodpeckers, Red-breasted Nuthatches, Hairy Woodpeckers, Red Crossbills and Pine Siskins.

CANYON TO TOWER-ROOSEVELT ROAD

Road Distance: 19 Miles/ 31 Kilometers

Road Map

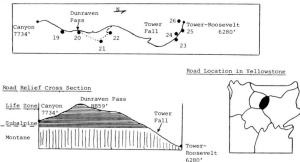

On the drive from Canyon to Tower-Roosevelt you will travel through two distinct life zones, the subalpine zone and the montane zone, and through a diversity of habitats. The change from one zone to the other is not that apparent but occurs in the vicinity of Tower Fall ㉓ . Starting at Canyon, the road climbs up a mountain pass. At the lower elevations keep an eye open for Steller's Jays. There are several pullouts on the Dunraven Road ⑲ —stop near the pass if you want to get an excellent view of the Grand Tetons to the south. This stop ⑲ and the stop at Dunraven Pass ⑳ are excellent places to observe Clark's Nutcrackers, Common Ravens, Cassin's Finches, and White-crowned Sparrows. A hike up to Mount Washburn ㉑ from either ⑳ or ㉒ , will sometimes yield a view of Rosy Finches and Water Pipits on the windswept summit. At the Antelope Creek overlook ㉒ look in the conifers for Townsend's Solitaires, Red Crossbills, Pine Siskins, and Cassin's Finches. Sometimes, if you are lucky, you may see a Blue Grouse along the wooded mountain ridges. As the road descends through open country, look for White-crowned Sparrows in the brushy draws. Red-tailed Hawks are also found in this open country. At Tower Fall ㉓ look for Tree Swallows and Steller's Jays. At the overhanging cliff area ㉔ look for White-throated Swifts, Violet-green Swallows, Cliff Swallows, and Tree Swallows. At Rainy Lake ㉕ look for Barrow's Goldeneyes and occasionally Ring-necked Ducks. Near Roosevelt Lodge ㉖ look for Red-breasted Nuthatches, Mountain Chickadees, Mountain Bluebirds, and Northern Flickers.

TOWER-ROOSEVELT TO NORTHEAST ENTRANCE ROAD

Road Distance: 29 Miles/ 47 Kilometers

Road Map

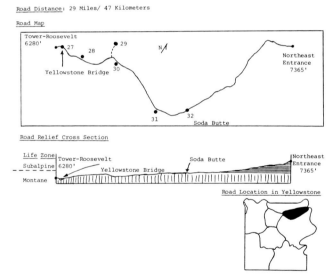

Road Relief Cross Section

Road Location in Yellowstone

You will experience a greater expanse of open habitats on this road than on any other road in Yellowstone. On the drive from Tower-Roosevelt to the Northeast Entrance you will travel through two distinct life zones, the montane zone and the subalpine zone. The change from one zone to another is not that apparent but occurs in the vicinity of Soda Butte ㉜ .

When heading from Tower-Roosevelt to the Northeast Entrance, a stop near the Yellowstone Bridge ㉗ is often rewarded with a look at Belted Kingfishers. Traveling farther east, you will find a hilly gravel landscape with numerous potholes and ponds, known as the Junction Butte ponds area ㉘ . Here you may observe Red-winged Blackbirds, Yellow-headed Blackbirds, American Coots, American Wigeon, Gadwalls, Cinnamon Teal, and Lesser Scaup. On the dry grasslands, where bison are often found, you can usually find Brown-headed Cowbirds. For a side tour, take the Slough Creek Drive ㉙ : in the small pothole country look for Cinnamon Teal, Ring-necked Ducks and Pied-billed Grebes, and near the Slough Creek campground search the conifers for Ruby-crowned Kinglets. Returning to the main road, continue eastward until you come to Lamar Canyon ㉚ . In the tall sagebrush look for Sage Thrashers, and along the fast-flowing Lamar River look for American Dippers. A stop at the Lamar Picnic Area ㉛ will sometimes give you a chance to see Spotted Sandpipers, Yellow Warblers, Lincoln's Sparrows and White-crowned Sparrows. The Lamar Valley is an excellent place to observe raptors such as American Kestrels, Prairie Falcons, and Golden Eagles. At Soda Butte ㉜ , look around and see if you can spot Golden Eagles. Farther east, past Pebble Creek campground, conifers border both sides of the road all the way to the Northeast Entrance. Ruby-crowned Kinglets and Yellow-rumped Warblers are easily found along this section of the road.

MAMMOTH TO TOWER-ROOSEVELT ROAD

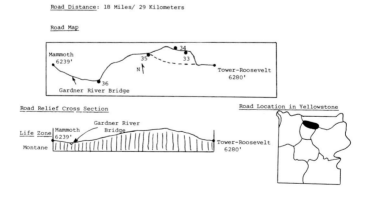

Road Distance: 18 Miles/ 29 Kilometers

Road Map

Road Relief Cross Section

Road Location in Yellowstone

This road lies entirely within the montane zone and passes through a wide variety of habitats. It is especially good for birding. Numerous stops at pullouts—and getting out of the car to investigate habitats—will produce excellent birding results.

Heading east from Mammoth to Tower-Roosevelt, a stop at the Gardner River bridge area could give you an opportunity to see Golden Eagles, Prairie Falcons, or Vesper Sparrows. At Lava Creek Picnic Area ㊱ look for American Dippers, Ruby-crowned Kinglets, American Robins, and Pine Siskins. In the open sagebrush areas look for Red-tailed Hawks, Vesper Sparrows, and Brewer's Sparrows. A side trip down the one-way Blacktail Plateau Drive ㉟ could give you a look at such birds as Red-naped Sapsuckers, Williamson's Sapsuckers, Tree Swallows, Red-breasted Nuthatches, Hairy Woodpeckers, Pine Siskins, Dusky Flycatchers, Blue Grouse, and Ruffed Grouse. There is a forest fire burn area ㉞ on the main road that is a fine place to observe cavity-nesting birds such as Three-toed Woodpeckers, Red-breasted Nuthatches, and Mountain Chickadees. At a small lake near the road, called Floating Island Lake ㉝ , you can usually find American Coots and Yellow-headed Blackbirds.

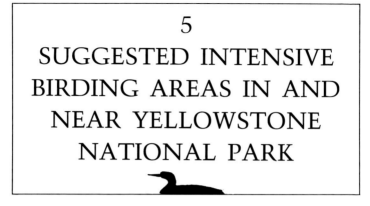

5
SUGGESTED INTENSIVE BIRDING AREAS IN AND NEAR YELLOWSTONE NATIONAL PARK

Of the countless places to watch birds in and around Yellowstone, the suggested intensive birding areas mentioned in this chapter will aid the birder in planning a birding trip. This chapter is divided into two parts: 1.) Suggested Intensive Birding Areas in Yellowstone National Park, and 2.) Suggested Intensive Birding Areas Near Yellowstone National Park. (Note: Since the greatest diversity of birds occurs in the summer, these generalizations about birds apply primarily to the summer months.)

SUGGESTED INTENSIVE BIRDING AREAS
IN YELLOWSTONE NATIONAL PARK

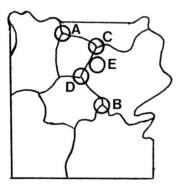

A. Mammoth
B. Fishing Bridge
C. Tower-Roosevelt
D. Canyon
E. Mount Washburn

Fig. 12. Suggested intensive birding areas in Yellowstone National Park.

There are numerous places to watch birds in Yellowstone. The five areas mentioned in this section truly represent the best birding areas in the Park. Whether you prefer to watch birds while in a vehicle or on a walk, these areas will provide you with the best overall sampling of the diversity of Yellowstone's vegetation and birdlife. This section will be especially helpful for those people with limited time in Yellowstone National Park (Figure 12).

A. Mammoth Area (Best time to visit: early May to early July; late August to late September.)

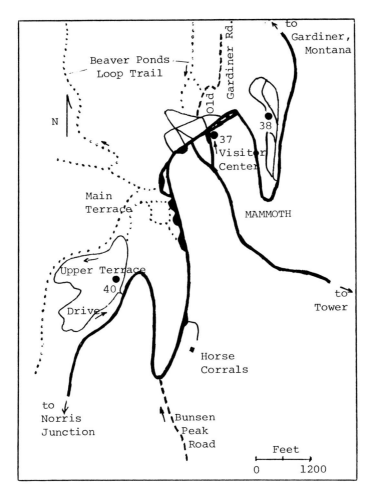

The *Mammoth* area is undoubtedly the best birding area in Yellowstone, whether in summer or winter. Although Mammoth itself is in the montane zone, within a ten mile radius you can find nearly all the major vegetation types represented in the Park. This is the only area in Yellowstone where all four life zones are found in proximity to one another – in traveling from the lower elevations near Gardiner, Montana, to the summit of Electric Peak, one passes through all four zones.

Some birds to look for in the summer: Red-tailed Hawk, Golden Eagle, Prairie Falcon, Killdeer, Red-naped Sapsucker, Williamson's Sapsucker, Hairy Woodpecker, Three-toed Woodpecker, Clark's Nutcracker, Black-billed Magpie, Common Raven, Mountain Chickadee, Red-breasted Nuthatch, Ruby-crowned Kinglet, Mountain Bluebird, Townsend's Solitaire, Yellow-rumped Warbler, Lazuli Bunting, Chipping Sparrow, Cassin's Finch, and Pine Siskin.

The following areas are recommended for birding:

Driving: Upper Terrace Drive, Old Gardiner Road, Mammoth-Gardiner Road, Bunsen Peak Road.

Walking: Main Terrace trails, Beaver Pond Loop Trail, Bunsen Peak Trail, Mammoth Museum-Headquarters area, Mammoth campground.

Red-naped   Yellow-bellied

The Yellow-bellied Sapsucker has been recently split into two distinct species: Red-naped Sapsucker and Yellow-bellied Sapsucker. The Red-naped Sapsucker is the species you are likely to encounter in Yellowstone.

B. Fishing Bridge Area   (Best time to visit: mid-May to mid-July; late August to early October.)

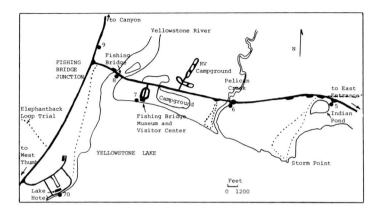

   The *Fishing Bridge Area* ranks high as a birding area, even though it is located completely in the subalpine zone. The complex mosaic of micro-environments contributes to the exceptional bird diversity found here. The Fishing Bridge Museum and vicinity is an excellent area for observing Yellowstone birdlife.

   Some birds to look for in the summer: Common Loon, American White Pelican, Canada Goose, Mallard, Green-winged Teal, Barrow's Goldeneye, Bufflehead, Common Merganser, Osprey, Bald Eagle, Swainson's Hawk, Spotted Sandpiper, Ring-billed Gull, California Gull, Caspian Tern, Common Tern, Belted Kingfisher, Tree Swallow, Common Raven, Mountain Chickadee, Ruby-crowned Kinglet, Yellow-rumped Warbler, Chipping Sparrow, Savannah Sparrow, Dark-eyed Junco, Brown-headed Cowbird, and Red Crossbill.

   The following areas are recommended for birding:
   Driving: Pelican Creek pullout, Indian Pond overlook, Fishing Bridge pullout, Lake Hotel waterfront.
   Walking: Fishing Bridge Museum and waterfront, Fishing Bridge, Elephant Back Loop Trail, Lake Hotel waterfront, Storm Point Loop Trail, Pelican Creek Nature Trail.

C. Tower-Roosevelt Area   (Best time to visit: mid-May to early July.)

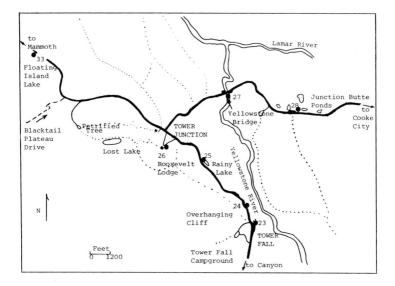

The Tower-Roosevelt area lies in the upper limits of the montane zone and is an excellent area for birdwatching in Yellowstone. The diverse array of vegetation contributes to the diversity of birdlife.

Some birds to look for in the summer: Ring-necked Duck, Ruddy Duck, Red-tailed Hawk, American Kestrel, Blue Grouse, Ruffed Grouse, Common Snipe, White-throated Swift, Red-naped Sapsucker, Williamson's Sapsucker, Downy Woodpecker, Hairy Woodpecker, Northern Flicker, Tree Swallow, Violet-green Swallow, Cliff Swallow, Steller's Jay, Clark's Nutcracker, Mountain Chickadee, Red-breasted Nuthatch, American Dipper, Ruby-crowned Kinglet, Mountain Bluebird, Yellow-rumped Warbler, Green-tailed Towhee, Chipping Sparrow, Brewer's Sparrow,

The Western Grebe has been recently split into two distinct species: Western Grebe (left) and Clark's Grebe (right).

Vesper Sparrow, Lincoln's Sparrow, White-crowned Sparrow, Dark-eyed Junco, Red-winged Blackbird, Western Meadowlark, Yellow-headed Blackbird, Brewer's Blackbird, and Pine Siskin.

The following areas are recommended for birding:

Driving: Tower to Tower Fall, Tower to Junction Butte ponds, Tower to Blacktail Plateau Drive, Blacktail Plateau Drive, Petrified Tree Drive.

Walking: Lost Lake Trail, Petrified Tree Trail, Tower Fall Trail, Roosevelt Lodge and vicinity, Yellowstone Picnic Trail, Garnet Hills-Hellroaring Trails.

D. Canyon Area (Best time to visit: early June to mid-July.)

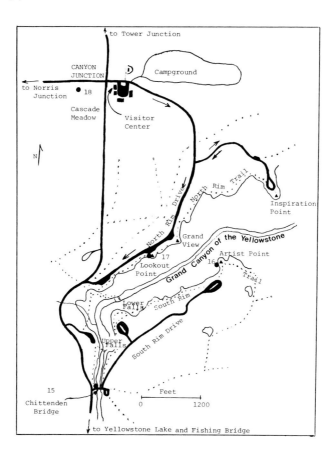

The *Canyon* area is one of the most spectacular places to watch birds in Yellowstone. It lies well within the subalpine zone, and although the birdlife is not as diverse as in other areas of the Park, what may be lost in bird variety is gained in spectacular scenery. The Grand Canyon of the Yellowstone is a remarkable place to watch birds: the vivid colors, the deep canyon walls, the spectacular waterfalls, will leave a lasting impression on your mind. The Canyon area is also the best place in Yellowstone to observe Ospreys on their nests, which are found on rock pinnacles.

Some birds to look for in the summer: Osprey, Swainson's Hawk, American Kestrel, Great Gray Owl, Northern Flicker, Violet-green Swallow, Cliff Swallow, Gray Jay, Clark's Nutcracker, Common Raven, Mountain Chickadee, Ruby-crowned Kinglet, Yellow-rumped Warbler, Western Tanager, Chipping Sparrow, Vesper Sparrow, Savannah Sparrow, White-crowned Sparrow, and Dark-eyed Junco.

The following areas are recommended for birding:

Driving: North Rim Drive, Inspiration Point Drive, South Rim Drive, Canyon-Hayden Valley Drive, Cascade Meadow.

Walking: North Rim Trail, South Rim Trail, Uncle Tom's Trail.

E. Mount Washburn Area   (Best time to visit: mid-June to mid-September.)

The *Mount Washburn* area is the only area in Yellowstone National Park where the visitor can easily approach the alpine zone. To experience the alpine environment, however, hiking is required. There are two parking areas located in the upper limits of the subalpine zone, from which trail heads lead to the alpine zone and the summit of Mount Washburn. One trail starts at the Antelope Creek overlook, and the other at Dunraven Pass. Not only is the hike to Mount Washburn an alpine experience, but it is one of the most spectacular areas from which to enjoy a panoramic view of Yellowstone National Park. It is a view you will never forget!

Some birds to look for in the summer:

Subalpine zone: Swainson's Hawk, Cooper's Hawk, Northern Goshawk, Blue Grouse, Hairy Woodpecker, Northern Flicker, Olive-sided Flycatcher, Tree Swallow,

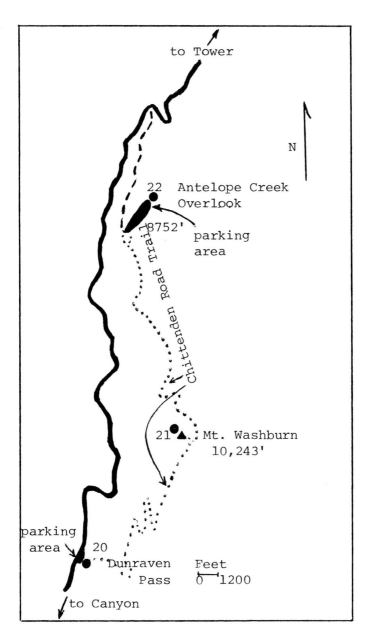

to Tower

N

22 Antelope Creek
    Overlook

8752'

parking
area

Chittenden Road Trail

21 ▲ Mt. Washburn
        10,243'

parking
area   20
          Dunraven
          Pass   Feet
                         0   1200
to Canyon

Violet-green Swallow, Gray Jay, Steller's Jay, Clark's Nutcracker, Common Raven, Mountain Chickadee, Ruby-crowned Kinglet, Mountain Bluebird, Townsend's Solitaire, Hermit Thrush, Yellow-rumped Warbler, Lincoln's Sparrow, White-crowned Sparrow, Dark-eyed Junco, Pine Grosbeak, and Cassin's Finch.

At timberline: Blue Grouse, Tree Swallow, Gray Jay, Clark's Nutcracker, Common Raven, Mountain Chickadee, Mountain Bluebird, Water Pipit, and White-crowned Sparrow.

Alpine zone: Golden Eagle, Peregrine Falcon, Prairie Falcon, Horned Lark, Common Raven, Rock Wren, Water Pipit, Rosy Finch.

The following areas are recommended for birding:

Driving: Antelope Creek overlook.

Walking: Chittenden Road Trail to Mount Washburn. *Note*: The hike to Mount Washburn is approximately three miles, with a minimum elevation gain of fifteen hundred feet. Time allotted for this birding hike should be two to four hours for the ascent and one to two hours for the descent to the parking areas. Since Mount Washburn is a high mountain summit, a rucksack or pack with warm clothing, food, and drinking water is highly encouraged.

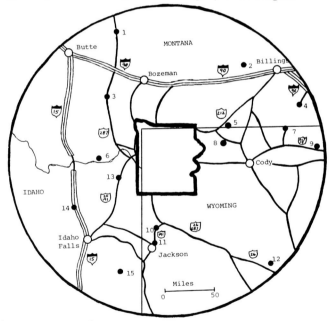

Fig. 13. Suggested intensive birding areas within 150-mile radius of Yellowstone National Park.

SUGGESTED INTENSIVE BIRDING AREAS
NEAR YELLOWSTONE NATIONAL PARK

Montana
1. Canyon Ferry Reservoir
2. Big Lake
3. Ennis Lake
4. Bighorn Canyon National Recreation Area (Yellowtail Dam Unit)
5. Beartooth Plateau (Custer National Forest)
6. Red Rock Lakes National Wildlife Refuge

Wyoming
7. Bighorn Canyon National Recreation Area (Horseshoe Bend Unit)
8. Sunlight Basin (Shoshone National Forest)
9. Shell Canyon (Bighorn National Forest)
10. Grand Teton National Park
11. National Elk Refuge
12. Ocean Lake

Idaho
13. Harriman State Park
14. Camas National Wildlife Refuge
15. Gray's Lake National Wildlife Refuge

6

A SUMMARY OF
ECOLOGICAL DATA ON
YELLOWSTONE BIRDS

TWO HUNDRED AND SEVENTY-NINE SPECIES OF birds have been observed in Yellowstone National Park since it was established in 1872. This chapter lists all species that have been documented and verified to occur in the Park. This information has been carefully scrutinized to eliminate as many misidentifications as possible. When reviewing historical bird records, it is extremely difficult to judge what was actually observed at the time. Many of the records prior to 1960 were accepted as is, unless there was a particular question of identification, time of year, or habitat. Prior to 1960 there were fewer amateur ornithologists, and those ornithologists probably made fewer misidentifications. After 1960 there was a substantial increase in amateur bird watchers and in the use of bird field guides, probably increasing the percentage of misidentifications. From 1960 to the present, unusual bird observations were not accepted unless substantiated with detailed field notes. In the future, it is hoped that individuals willing to contribute bird information will kindly take the time to submit detailed descriptions of rare and unusual birds they happen to see.

Bird abundance is perhaps one of the most difficult-to-measure aspects of ornithology. Much of the problem lies in the great variation in our knowledge, or lack of knowledge, of the different species. Through time, ornithologists are finding out that some species once considered uncommon are in fact quite common, now that their habitat requirements and life strategies are better understood. However, there is still a great deal to be learned about the more secretive species of birds in Yellowstone and throughout North America.

YELLOWSTONE BIRD CHECKLIST
AND ECOLOGICAL CHARTS
Those birds listed in the Yellowstone Bird Checklist and Ecological Charts are birds you are likely to encounter on a trip to Yellowstone National Park. This section is designed to provide as much information in graphic form as possible about Yellowstone's birds. The symbols in the charts are interpreted as follows:

Breeding Status
■ Confirmed breeder; nests, eggs, or young have been observed.
□ Migrants, visitors, accidentals.
H Historical breeding evidence only; not reported nesting in recent years.

Overall Abundance
A Abundant: can be encountered without much effort in the appropriate habitat.
C Common: can be encountered in the appropriate habitat but may require some effort in looking and/ or listening.
U Uncommon: these birds are not enountered every day, but one or more sightings are possible with diligent searching in the appropriate habitat.
R Rare: seldom encountered by Park visitors, even experienced birders; you will need luck as well as good eyes to find this species, even in the appropriate habitat.

Monthly Occurrence The months of the year a particular bird is likely to be encountered in Yellowstone. Data based on actual arrival and departure data.

Monthly Abundance
▬▬▬ Abundant
▬▬▬ Common
▬▬▬ Uncommon
● Rare (Occasionally observed during this month)

Life Zones The life zone(s) the particular bird frequents in Yellowstone.

Habitat Birds are typically found within one or more

of these three basic habitat types of a particular life zone: water, open, forested.

Best Area(s)   Numbers refer to the index map of Yellowstone's best birding areas.

Best Month(s)   The best month(s) of the year to find this particular bird in Yellowstone.

Chances of Finding the Bird   Given the checklist and ecological chart data, the chances of finding this bird in Yellowstone can be graded: excellent, moderate, difficult.

Request Additional Information   + More information is needed on the life history of this species in Yellowstone. If you have observations of this bird, please contact Yellowstone National Park.

Unusual: these birds have been accepted into Yellowstone National Park records but are not encountered very often. They are considered unusual because they are either out of their normal range or in highly restrictive habitat types. Italicized species are known to have nested in Yellowstone in the past.

Red-throated Loon
Pacific Loon
Great Egret
Wood Stork
Greater White-fronted Goose
Brant
American Black Duck
Eurasian Wigeon
Greater Scaup
Oldsquaw
Black Scoter
Surf Scoter
White-winged Scoter
Crested Caracara (probable escapee)
Sage Grouse
Gray Partridge
White-tailed Ptarmigan
Sharp-tailed Grouse
Snowy Plover
Mountain Plover
Upland Sandpiper
Ruddy Turnstone
Herring Gull
Sabine's Gull
Black-billed Cuckoo

White-headed Woodpecker
Pileated Woodpecker
Least Flycatcher
Gray Flycatcher
Ash-throated Flycatcher
Cassin's Kingbird
Blue Jay
Canyon Wren
Winter Wren
Western Bluebird
Varied Thrush
Brown Thrasher
Northern Mockingbird
Sprague's Pipit
Phainopepla
Tennessee Warbler
Nashville Warbler
Virginia's Warbler
Cape May Warbler
Blackpoll Warbler
Prothonotary Warbler
Ovenbird
Scarlet Tanager
Rose-breasted Grosbeak
Field Sparrow

Snowy Owl
Northern Hawk-Owl
Boreal Owl
Red-headed Woodpecker

Black-chinned Sparrow
Sage Sparrow
Baird's Sparrow
Swamp Sparrow
White-throated Sparrow
Bobolink
House Finch

Hypothetical: these birds have been reported in Yellowstone National Park but the documentation was inadequate and consequently considered unacceptable for Park records

Smew
Spruce Grouse
Hudsonian Godwit
Short-billed Dowitcher
American Woodcock
Least Tern
Common Barn Owl
Barred Owl
Ruby-throated Hummingbird
Philadelphia Vireo
Indigo Bunting
Clay-colored Sparrow
Scott's Oriole
Purple Finch

Unreliable: these birds have been reported in Yellowstone National Park without any detailed documentation whatsoever; the reports are questionable and are considered unacceptable for Park records

Black Swift
Black-chinned Hummingbird
Bendire's Thrasher
Blackburnian Warbler
Le Conte's Sparrow
Tri-colored Blackbird

Yellowstone Bird Checklist and Ecological Charts

Species	Breeding Status	Overall Abundance	Best Area(s)	Best Month(s)	Chances of observing this bird	Additional Data Need
Common Loon	■	U	3,4	5,10	Moderate	+
Pied-billed Grebe	■	U	28,29	5,6	Difficult	+
Horned Grebe	H	R	13,71	5,6	Difficult	+
Red-necked Grebe		R	13,71	6,7	Difficult	+
Eared Grebe	■	U	13,28	5,6	Moderate	+
Clark's Grebe		R	6,71	6,7	Difficult	+
Western Grebe	■	U	6,13	5,6	Moderate	+
American White Pelican	■	C	8,11	5,6	Moderate	
Double-crested Cormorant	■	U	3,8	6,7	Moderate	
American Bittern		R	6,12	6,7	Difficult	+
Great Blue Heron	■	U	8,56	6,7	Moderate	
Snowy Egret		R	8,13	6,9	Difficult	+
Black-crowned Night-Heron		R	6,13	5,6	Difficult	+
White-faced Ibis		R	5,13	5,6	Difficult	+
Tundra Swan		U	6,8	10,11	Moderate	+
Trumpeter Swan	■	C	4,56	6,7	Excellent	
Snow Goose		R	6,13	4,10	Difficult	+

Habitat (Water): all listed species marked "W".

Life Zone(s): marks primarily in Montane (and some Subalpine).

Yellowstone Bird Checklist and Ecological Charts

Life Zone(s) Habitat

Species	Breeding Status	Overall Abundance	Monthly Occurrence and Abundance (J F M A M J J A S O N D)	Foothills	Montane	Subalpine	Alpine	Forested	Open	Water	Best Area(s)	Best Month(s)	Chances of observing this bird	Need Additional Data
Canada Goose	■	A								W	12,56	6,7	Excellent	
Wood Duck	H	R								W	28,64	5,9	Difficult	+
Green-winged Teal	■	C								W	6,45	5,6	Excellent	
Mallard	■	A								W	13,56	6,7	Excellent	
Northern Pintail	■	U								W	11,13	5,6	Moderate	
Blue-winged Teal	■	U								W	6,28	6,7	Moderate	
Cinnamon Teal	■	C								W	6,45	5,6	Moderate	
Northern Shoveler	■	U								W	6,13	5,6	Moderate	
Gadwall	■	C								W	13,28	6,7	Moderate	
American Wigeon	■	C								W	6,13	6,7	Excellent	
Canvasback		U								W	4,6	6,10	Moderate	+
Redhead	■	U								W	4,6	6,7	Moderate	+
Ring-necked Duck	■	C								W	25,28	5,6	Excellent	
Lesser Scaup	■	C								W	6,28	6,7	Excellent	
Harlequin Duck	■	R								W	10,27	5,6	Difficult	+
Common Goldeneye		U								W	8,13	2,11	Excellent	
Barrow's Goldeneye	■	A								W	1,8	6,7	Excellent	

Yellowstone Bird Checklist and Ecological Charts

Species	Breeding Status	Overall Abundance	Forested	Open	Water	Best Area(s)	Best Month(s)	Chances of observing this bird	Need Additional Data
Bufflehead		U			W	6,8	6,7	Excellent	
Hooded Merganser		R			W	8,13	6,9	Difficult	+
Common Merganser	■	C			W	8,11	6,7	Excellent	
Red-breasted Merganser		R			W	8,13	6,9	Difficult	+
Ruddy Duck	■	U			W	28,33	5,6	Moderate	
Turkey Vulture		R		O	W	31,32	6,8	Difficult	+
Osprey	■	C		O	W	16,17	7,8	Excellent	
Bald Eagle	■	U	F	O	W	6,13	5,6	Moderate	
Northern Harrier	■	U		O		13,28	6,9	Difficult	+
Sharp-shinned Hawk	■	U	F	O		26,48	5,6	Moderate	+
Cooper's Hawk	■	U	F	O		23,35	6,7	Moderate	+
Northern Goshawk	■	U	F	O		35,42	5,6	Moderate	+
Swainson's Hawk	■	C	F	O		11,18	6,7	Moderate	
Red-tailed Hawk	■	C		O		24,39	5,6	Excellent	
Ferruginous Hawk		R		O		31,32	8,9	Difficult	+
Rough-legged Hawk		U		O		13,31	9,10	Difficult	+
Golden Eagle	■	U		O		32,39	5,6	Moderate	

Life Zone(s): Foothills, Montane, Subalpine, Alpine — Habitat

Monthly Occurrence and Abundance: J F M A M J J A S O N D

Yellowstone Bird Checklist and Ecological Charts

Species	Breeding Status	Overall Abundance	Foothills	Montane	Subalpine	Alpine	Forested	Open	Water	Best Area(s)	Best Month(s)	Chances of observing this bird	Need Additional Data
American Kestrel	■	C					F	O		31,35	5,6	Excellent	
Merlin	H	R					F	O		37,38	3,4	Difficult	+
Peregrine Falcon	■	R					F	O	W	12,13	5,6	Difficult	+
Prairie Falcon		U						O		32,39	6,7	Moderate	
Blue Grouse	■	C					F	O		22,35	6,7	Moderate	
Ruffed Grouse	■	U					F	O		35,42	5,6	Moderate	
Yellow Rail		R							W	6,61	7,8	Difficult	+
Virginia Rail		R							W	6,61	7,8	Difficult	+
Sora		C							W	6,61	6,7	Moderate	
American Coot	■	C							W	28,33	6,7	Excellent	
Sandhill Crane	■	U						O		11,59	5,6	Moderate	
Whooping Crane		R						O		-,75	6,7	Difficult	+
Black-bellied Plover		R							W	6,13	7,8	Difficult	+
Semipalmated Plover		R							W	6,13	7,8	Difficult	+
Killdeer	■	C						O	W	13,40	6,7	Excellent	
Black-necked Stilt		R							W	4,6	5,6	Difficult	+
American Avocet		U							W	6,8	6,7	Moderate	+

Monthly Occurrence and Abundance (J F M A M J J A S O N D)

Life Zone(s)   Habitat

Yellowstone Bird Checklist and Ecological Charts

Species	Breeding Status	Overall Abundance	Life Zone(s)	Habitat (Forested/Open/Water)	Best Area(s)	Best Month(s)	Chances of observing this bird	Need Additional Data
Greater Yellowlegs		R	Montane	W	6,13	8,9	Moderate	+
Lesser Yellowlegs		R	Montane	W	6,13	8,9	Moderate	+
Solitary Sandpiper		R	Montane	W	8,14	8,9	Moderate	+
Willet	■	U	Montane	W	4,6	5,6	Moderate	+
Spotted Sandpiper	■	C	Foothills, Montane	F O W	8,64	6,7	Excellent	
Long-billed Curlew	H	R	Foothills	O	12,13	6,7	Difficult	+
Marbled Godwit	■	R	Montane	O W	6,71	6,7	Moderate	+
Sanderling		R	Montane	W	4,64	5,9	Difficult	+
Semipalmated Sandpiper		U	Montane	W	6,13	7,8	Difficult	+
Western Sandpiper		R	Montane	W	6,13	8,9	Difficult	+
Least Sandpiper		R	Montane	W	6,13	8,9	Difficult	+
Baird's Sandpiper		R	Montane	W	6,13	7,8	Difficult	+
Pectoral Sandpiper		R	Montane	W	6,13	7,8	Difficult	+
Long-billed Dowitcher		U	Montane	W	6,13	6,8	Moderate	+
Common Snipe	■	C	Montane	W	6,12	5,6	Excellent	
Wilson's Phalarope	■	U	Montane	W	13,28	6,7	Moderate	+
Red-necked Phalarope		R	Montane	W	13,28	5,8	Difficult	+

Yellowstone Bird Checklist and Ecological Charts

Species	Breeding Status	Overall Abundance	Monthly Occurrence and Abundance	Life Zone(s)	Habitat	Best Area(s)	Best Month(s)	Chances of observing this bird	Need Additional Data
Franklin's Gull		R	J–A (Montane/Subalpine)	Montane, Subalpine	W	6,11	6,7	Difficult	+
Bonaparte's Gull		R	A–M	Montane, Subalpine	W	4,6	5,–	Difficult	+
Ring-billed Gull	■	U		Montane, Subalpine	W	6,8	6,7	Moderate	
California Gull	■	A		Montane, Subalpine	W	6,8	6,7	Excellent	
Caspian Tern	■	U		Montane, Subalpine	W	4,6	6,7	Moderate	+
Common Tern	■	U		Montane, Subalpine	W	4,6	5,6	Moderate	+
Forster's Tern		R		Montane, Subalpine	W	4,6	5,6	Difficult	+
Black Tern	■	H / R	M–S	Montane, Subalpine	W	4,6	5,6	Difficult	+
Rock Dove		U	J–D	Foothills	O	37,39	5,6	Moderate	
Mourning Dove		U	A–O	Foothills, Montane	O	25,26	6,7	Moderate	
Western Screech-Owl	■	R	J–D	Montane	F	31,44	6,7	Difficult	+
Great Horned Owl	■	U	J–D	Montane	F, O	38,40	4,5	Moderate	+
Northern Pygmy-Owl	■	R	J–D	Montane	F	36,39	12,1	Difficult	+
Burrowing Owl		H / R	A–O	Montane	O	29,32	4,5	Difficult	+
Great Gray Owl	■	U	J–D	Montane	F, O	18,33	6,7	Difficult	+
Long-eared Owl	■	R	A–D	Montane	F, O	39,40	6,7	Difficult	+
Short-eared Owl	■	R	A–D	Montane	O	6,13	7,8	Difficult	+

Yellowstone Bird Checklist and Ecological Charts

Species	Breeding Status	Overall Abundance	Life Zone(s): Foothills	Montane	Subalpine	Alpine	Habitat: Forested	Open	Water	Best Area(s)	Best Month(s)	Chances of observing this bird	Need Additional Data
Northern Saw-whet Owl	■	R					F			35,42	6,7	Difficult	+
Common Nighthawk	■	C						O		38,39	6,7	Moderate	
White-throated Swift	■	U					F	O		24,42	6,7	Excellent	+
Calliope Hummingbird	■	C					F	O		26,33	7,8	Difficult	+
Broad-tailed Hummingbird	■	R					F	O		26,29	7,8	Difficult	+
Rufous Hummingbird	■	U					F	O		26,36	7,8	Difficult	+
Belted Kingfisher	■	U							W	10,39	5,6	Excellent	
Lewis' Woodpecker	H	R					F	O		23,35	5,6	Difficult	+
Red-naped Sapsucker	■	C					F			35,42	5,6	Excellent	+
Williamson's Sapsucker	■	U					F			23,35	6,7	Moderate	+
Downy Woodpecker	■	U					F			38,39	6,7	Moderate	+
Hairy Woodpecker	■	C					F			23,38	6,7	Excellent	+
Three-toed Woodpecker	■	U					F			38,40	6,7	Moderate	+
Black-backed Woodpecker	■	R					F			46,64	6,7	Difficult	+
Northern Flicker	■	C					F	O		26,62	6,7	Excellent	
Olive-sided Flycatcher	■	U					F			23,35	6,7	Difficult	+
Western Wood-Pewee	■	U					F			23,29	6,7	Moderate	+

Yellowstone Bird Checklist and Ecological Charts

Species	Breeding Status	Overall Abundance	Monthly Occurrence and Abundance	Life Zone(s)	Habitat (Forested / Open / Water)	Best Area(s)	Best Month(s)	Chances of observing this bird	Need Additional Data
Willow Flycatcher	■	U			F	29,43	6,7	Difficult	+
Hammond's Flycatcher	■	U			F	35,42	6,7	Moderate	+
Dusky Flycatcher	■	C			F	29,42	6,7	Moderate	+
Western Flycatcher	■	R			F	40,41	6,7	Difficult	+
Say's Phoebe	H	R			O	41,48	6,7	Difficult	+
Western Kingbird	H	R			O	29,39	7,8	Difficult	+
Eastern Kingbird	H	R			O	29,39	6,7	Difficult	+
Horned Lark	■	U			O	21,35	6,7	Moderate	
Tree Swallow	■	A			O	24,42	6,7	Excellent	
Violet-green Swallow	■	C			O	17,24	6,7	Excellent	
Northern Rough-winged Swallow	■	U			O	11,39	6,7	Moderate	
Bank Swallow	■	U			O	4,11	6,7	Moderate	
Cliff Swallow	■	A			O	11,38	6,7	Excellent	
Barn Swallow	■	U			O	26,37	6,7	Excellent	
Gray Jay	■	C			F	14,69	8,9	Excellent	
Steller's Jay	■	U			F	20,23	6,7	Moderate	
Pinyon Jay		R			F O	38,40	11,12	Difficult	+

Yellowstone Bird Checklist and Ecological Charts

Species	Breeding Status	Overall Abundance	Forested	Open	Water	Best Area(s)	Best Month(s)	Chances of observing this bird	Need Additional Data
Clark's Nutcracker	■	A	F	O		20,40	6,7	Excellent	
Black-billed Magpie	■	C		O		38,39	5,6	Excellent	
American Crow	■	R		O		38,39	6,7	Moderate	
Common Raven	■	A	F	O	W	16,62	6,7	Excellent	
Black-capped Chickadee	■	U	F			38,39	6,7	Moderate	
Mountain Chickadee	■	A	F			7,35	5,6	Excellent	
Red-breasted Nuthatch	■	C	F			38,40	6,7	Excellent	
White-breasted Nuthatch	■	U	F			38,40	6,7	Moderate	
Pygmy Nuthatch		R	F			23,38	6,9	Difficult	+
Brown Creeper	■	R	F			38,40	5,6	Difficult	
Rock Wren	■	C		O		36,41	5,6	Excellent	
House Wren	■	C	F			29,42	6,7	Moderate	
Marsh Wren	■	R			W	6,8	6,7	Difficult	+
American Dipper	■	C			W	53,58	5,6	Excellent	
Golden-crowned Kinglet	■	U	F			45,64	6,7	Difficult	
Ruby-crowned Kinglet	■	C	F			35,42	6,7	Excellent	+
Mountain Bluebird	■	C	F	O		26,40	5,6	Excellent	

Life Zone(s): Foothills, Montane, Subalpine, Alpine

Habitat

ECOLOGICAL DATA

Yellowstone Bird Checklist and Ecological Charts

Species	Breeding Status	Overall Abundance	Monthly Occurrence and Abundance (J F M A M J J A S O N D)	Life Zone(s) (Foothills / Montane / Subalpine / Alpine)	Habitat Forested	Habitat Open	Habitat Water	Best Area(s)	Best Month(s)	Chances of observing this bird	Additional Data Need
Townsend's Solitaire	■	U			F			40,42	6,7	Moderate	
Veery	H	R			F			23,42	6,7	Difficult	+
Swainson's Thrush	■	C			F			23,42	6,7	Moderate	
Hermit Thrush	■	C			F			23,42	6,7	Moderate	
American Robin	■	A			F	O		37,70	6,7	Excellent	+
Gray Catbird	■	R				O		39,–	6,7	Difficult	+
Sage Thrasher	■	U				O		29,35	6,7	Moderate	+
Water Pipit	■	C				O		21,–	7,8	Excellent	
Bohemian Waxwing		U			F			37,39	11,12	Moderate	+
Cedar Waxwing		U			F			26,27	5,6	Moderate	+
Northern Shrike		U				O		31,32	3,10	Moderate	+
Loggerhead Shrike		R				O		31,32	5,6	Difficult	+
European Starling	■	C			F	O		26,29	5,6	Excellent	
Solitary Vireo		R			F			23,26	6,7	Difficult	+
Warbling Vireo	■	C			F			35,37	6,7	Excellent	
Red-eyed Vireo		R			F			38,39	8,9	Difficult	+
Orange-crowned Warbler	H	R			F			38,39	5,6	Difficult	+

Yellowstone Bird Checklist and Ecological Charts

Species	Breeding Status	Overall Abundance	Monthly Occurrence and Abundance (J F M A M J J A S O N D)	Life Zone(s): Foothills	Montane	Subalpine	Alpine	Habitat: Forested	Open	Water	Best Area(s)	Best Month(s)	Chances of observing this bird	Need Additional Data
Yellow Warbler	■	C						F			37,75	5,6	Excellent	
Yellow-rumped Warbler	■	A						F			17,64	5,6	Excellent	
Townsend's Warbler	■	R						F			40,64	5,6	Difficult	+
American Redstart	H	R						F			39,75	5,6	Difficult	+
Northern Waterthrush		R						F		W	6,64	5,6	Difficult	+
MacGillivray's Warbler	■	C						F		W	39,42	5,6	Moderate	
Common Yellowthroat	■	C						F		W	6,39	5,6	Excellent	
Wilson's Warbler	■	U						F		W	43,50	5,6	Moderate	
Western Tanager	■	C						F			23,42	6,7	Excellent	
Black-headed Grosbeak		R						F			38,42	6,7	Difficult	+
Lazuli Bunting		C							O		38,39	6,7	Moderate	
Green-tailed Towhee		U							O		39,41	6,7	Moderate	
Rufous-sided Towhee		R							O		38,39	6,7	Difficult	+
American Tree Sparrow		U							O		37,38	10,11	Moderate	
Chipping Sparrow	■	C						F	O		23,38	6,7	Excellent	
Brewer's Sparrow	■	C							O		32,35	6,7	Excellent	
Vesper Sparrow	■	C							O		35,39	6,7	Excellent	

154

Yellowstone Bird Checklist and Ecological Charts

Species	Breeding Status	Overall Abundance	Forested	Open	Water	Best Area(s)	Best Month(s)	Chances of observing this bird	Need Additional Data
Lark Sparrow	H	R		O		31,45	6,7	Difficult	✚
Lark Bunting		R		O		31,32	6,7	Difficult	✚
Savannah Sparrow	■	C		O		13,51	6,7	Excellent	
Grasshopper Sparrow		R		O		30,31	6,7	Difficult	✚
Fox Sparrow	■	R	F	O		38,39	5,6	Difficult	✚
Song Sparrow	■	U		O		39,75	5,6	Moderate	
Lincoln's Sparrow	■	C	F	O		31,50	6,7	Excellent	
White-crowned Sparrow	■	C	F	O		3,20	6,7	Excellent	
Harris' Sparrow		R		O		37,38	10,11	Difficult	✚
Dark-eyed Junco	■	A	F			23,52	6,7	Excellent	
McCown's Longspur		R		O		39,–	5,9	Difficult	✚
Lapland Longspur		R		O		39,–	3,12	Difficult	✚
Snow Bunting		R		O		32,39	3,12	Difficult	✚
Red-winged Blackbird	■	C		O	W	28,29	6,7	Excellent	
Western Meadowlark	■	C		O		30,32	5,6	Excellent	
Yellow-headed Blackbird	■	C		O	W	28,33	5,6	Excellent	
Brewer's Blackbird	■	C		O		26,38	6,7	Excellent	

Yellowstone Bird Checklist and Ecological Charts

Species	Breeding Status	Overall Abundance	Monthly Occurrence and Abundance	Life Zone(s): Foothills	Montane	Subalpine	Alpine	Habitat: Forested	Open	Water	Best Area(s)	Best Month(s)	Chances of observing this bird	Need Additional Data
Common Grackle		R							O		38,39	5,6	Difficult	+
Brown-headed Cowbird	■	C							O		11,13	5,6	Excellent	
Northern Oriole	H	R						F			31,37	5,6	Difficult	+
Rosy Finch	■	U							O		21,38	2,3	Moderate	
Pine Grosbeak	■	U						F			71,72	6,7	Moderate	+
Cassin's Finch	■	C						F			38,70	5,6	Excellent	
Red Crossbill	■	U						F			7,54	6,7	Moderate	
White-winged Crossbill		R						F			73,74	7,8	Difficult	+
Common Redpoll		R							O		38,39	3,12	Difficult	+
Hoary Redpoll		R							O		38,39	1,12	Difficult	+
Pine Siskin	■	C						F	O		37,38	5,6	Excellent	
American Goldfinch	H	R							O		38,39	8,9	Difficult	+
Evening Grosbeak	■	U						F			38,42	6,7	Moderate	+
House Sparrow		R							O		37,38	6,7	Difficult	+

EPILOGUE

Birdwatching is much more than the art of bird identification – it is the art of discovering how birds live in relation to their physical and biological environment. Making new discoveries about birds is not something of the past but is very much possible today. Of all the sciences, ornithology is one of the few to which amateurs can and do make significant contributions to scientific knowledge. Visitors are encouraged to submit accurate and detailed observations about Yellowstone birds, particularly those species for which additional information is badly needed. All carefully documented bird information will be incorporated into subsequent printings of this field guide and will represent the most up-to-date information on Yellowstone's birds.

A total of 279 species of birds has been recorded thus far in Yellowstone. Even though the bird species total is not so impressive compared with other areas of the world, it is still remarkable when the altitude and extreme climate are considered. The diversity of Yellowstone's birdlife is a direct reflection of the diversity of the habitat. Yellowstone is one of the most impressive wilderness areas in the world. Although humans have made their mark on its natural resources, it is important to realize that we are only visitors and that our impact must be kept to a minimum. For Yellowstone is truly one of the greatest conservatories of America's wildlife.

Glossary of Terms

alpine zone: an altitudinal or life zone found in Yellowstone between 10,000 feet and 11,385 feet in elevation; the treeless area above timberline also referred to as the "Arctic zone."

attitude: distinct posture of a particular species of bird.

cere: a bare, often colorful, fleshy area that surrounds the nostrils on the upper mandible.

ecology: the study of mutual relationships between organisms and their environment.

ecosystem: the area required for total natural ecological relationships to take place with a minimum of interference by humans.

ecotone: the overlap of one plant community with another.

environment: the surroundings in which an organism resides.

flanks: the sides of a bird's body, located below the wings and slightly to the rear.

foothills zone: an altitudinal or life zone found in Yellowstone between 5,280 feet and 6,000 feet in elevation, sometimes referred to as the "Transition zone."

gape: the opening between the upper and lower mandibles; the opening of the mouth.

habitat: a place where an animal dwells.

hybridize: to crossbreed; to interbreed,

jizz: a term derived from a British fighter pilots acronym GIS, which stands for general impression and shape; most recently it has been regarded as the holistic method of birding, which combines a bird's general impression and shape and/or distinct behavioral traits.

life zone: the relationship of plant and animal communities based on topography, climate, and elevation; an altitudinal zone.

lores: the area between the eye and the base of the bill.

mnemonic: assisting the memory; an organized system used in memory training.

montane zone: an altitudinal or life zone found in Yellowstone between 6,000 feet and 7,600 feet in elevation; also referred to as the "Canadian zone."

nape: the back of the neck.

niche: the "profession" of a bird, or what it does for a living; the role of a bird within plant and animal communities is a result of structural, physiological, psychological, and behavioral adaptations.

ornithology: the study of birds.

pampas: vast treeless plains, such as the pampas of Argentina.

profile: a silhouette; a biographical sketch.

raptor(s): a group of carnivorous birds or birds of prey consisting of hawks, falcons, eagles, vultures, and owls, known for their rapacious means of obtaining prey.

riparian: the habitat closely associated with the bank of a stream, river, or lake.

silhouette: a representation of an outline of an object, often appearing as one dark uniform color; a profile.

species: a group of animals or plants which possess in common one or more distinctive characteristics, and do or may interbreed and reproduce their characteristics in their offspring; a distinct kind of plant or animal.

subalpine zone: an altitudinal or life zone found in Yellowstone between 7,600 feet and 10,000 feet in elevation; also referred to as the "Hudsonian zone."

territory: an area that is usually defended against other members of the same species, which usually contains a nest site, food, or both.

timberline: the boundary between the subalpine and alpine zones; at this elevational boundary timber ceases to grow.

ungulate(s): hoofed mammals such as elk, moose, deer, etc.

Acknowledgements

It would be impossible to mention all the people who have contributed to this book. However without the help and encouragement of the following individuals, this book would never have materialized.

—Chief Park Naturalist George Robinson provided perhaps the most valuable assistance. He believed in the concept of the book. His continued support, comments, editorial review, and communication throughout the writing of this manuscript was greatly appreciated.
—Larry Thompson made extremely valuable contributions by providing life-history information, historical data, editorial review, book layout ideas, and moral support. His extraordinary expertise was greatly appreciated.
—Former Resource Management Specialist Ken Czarnowski and Research Chief John Varley provided invaluable assistance in the form of moral support, suggestions, and manuscript review from the inception of the book until the completion of the final product.
—Superintendent Bob Barbee, Chief Ranger Dan Sholly, Assistant Chief Ranger Gary Brown, were extremely cooperative and supportive.
—Research Botanist Don Despain provided valuable data and comments on the habitat sections.
—The following Yellowstone National Park personnel were extremely helpful in providing either field assistance, data, editorial comments, or suggestions: Lona

Flocke, Steve Flocke, Bill Laitner, Tim Manns, Bill Schreier, and Joe Zarki.

—The following people provided additional data and/or editorial comments on the manuscript: John Craighead, Rod Drewien, Dick Follett, Bill Heinrich, Bob Oakleaf, Sharon Ritter, Jon Swenson and Daryl Tessen.

—Jon Dunn graciously edited the manuscript and provided excellent suggestions regarding species identification and book layout.

—Gerry and Laurette Maisel kindly edited the manuscript and provided valuable suggestions regarding book content, book layout, and species identification.

—Wildlife Photographers Jerry Craig, Frank Oberle, Bob Twist, and Mike Quinton provided many of the beautiful photographs.

—Nancy Breuninger for typing the manuscript.

—Rick Rinehart of Roberts-Rinehart Publishers (Boulder, Colo.) for his unending assistance with all aspects of the book from start to finish.

—Debbie Broaddus for her editorial review of the manuscript.

—The park rangers of Yellowstone National Park for their dedication and commitment of protecting the Park resources, and for providing information over the years.

—I wish to express my appreciation to my family and friends for their unending support to complete such a book.

—My wife, Karen McEneaney, provided the stimulus, moral support, and understanding needed to complete the book. Her excellent artistic ideas, bird drawings and silhouettes have contributed greatly to this book.

—Finally, I wish to thank all bird watchers who have contributed their accurate and detailed bird observations to Yellowstone National Park. A book such as this can only be accomplished through a group effort.

Bibliography

Bailey, V. 1930. Animal Life of Yellowstone National Park. Springfield, Illinois: Charles C. Thomas.

Bent, A.C. 1915-1968. Life Histories of North American Birds. New York: Dover Publications.

Coues, E. 1874. Birds of the Northwest: a handbook of ornithology of the region drained by the Missouri River and its tributaries. Misc. Publ. No. 3. Washington, D.C.: U.S. Geological Survey of Territories.

Despain, D.G. 1973. Major Vegetative Zones of Yellowstone National Park. Information Paper No. 19, Yellowstone National Park, U.S.D.I. National Park Service.

Diem, K.L. and D.D. Condon. 1967. Breeding Studies of Water Birds on the Molly Islands (Yellowstone Lake, Wyoming). Yellowstone Library and Museum Association. U.S.D.I. National Park Service.

Drewien, R., W. Brown, and J. Varley. 1985. The Greater Sandhill Crane in Yellowstone National Park: A Preliminary Survey. Grand Island, Nebraska: 1985 Crane Workshop Proceedings.

Farrand, J. Jr. 1983. The Audubon Society: Master Guide to Birding. Vols. 1,2,3. New York: Alfred Knopf.

Follett, D. 1986. Birds of Yellowstone and Grand Teton National Parks. Yellowstone Library and Museum Association. Boulder, Colorado: Roberts Rinehart, Inc.

Grinnel, G.B. 1876. Report of the Reconnaissance from Carroll, Montana, to the Yellowstone National Park and Return, by William Ludlow. Washington D.C.: Government Printing Office.

Grinnell, J. and T.I. Storer. 1924. Animal Life in the Yosemite. Berkeley, California: University of California Press.

Gruson, E.S. 1972. Words for Birds, A Lexicon of North American

Birds with Biographical Notes. New York: Quadrangle Books.

Keefer, W.R. 1984. The Geologic History of Yellowstone National Park. Yellowstone Library and Museum Association. U.S.D.I. National Park Service.

Kemsies, E. 1930. Birds of Yellowstone National Park. Wilson Bulletin, 42:198-210 (September) pp. 198-210.

Kortright, F.H. 1942. The Ducks, Geese, and Swans of North America. Harrisburg, Pennsylvania: The Stackpole Co., and Washington, D.C.: The Wildlife Management Institute.

Knight, W.C. 1902. The Birds of Wyoming. Laramie, Wyoming: University of Wyoming Agriculture Experiment Station Bulletin No. 55.

Mearns, E.A. 1903. Feathers Beside the Styx. Condor (March): 37-39.

Merriam, C.H. 1873. "Birds". U.S. Geological Survey of Territories by F.V. Hayden. Washington, D.C.

McCreary, O. 1939. Wyoming Bird Life. Minneapolis, Minnesota: Burgess Publ. Co.

Murie, A. 1940. Ecology of the Coyote in Yellowstone. Fauna Series No. 1, Conservation Bull. No. 4. Washington, D.C.: U.S. Government Printing Office.

Newton, I. 1979. Population Ecology of Raptors. Vermillion, South Dakota: Buteo Books.

Oakleaf, B., H. Downing, B. Raynes, M. Raynes, and O. Scott. 1982. Wyoming Avian Atlas. Lander, Wyoming: Wyoming Game and Fish Department.

Odum, E. 1959. Fundamentals of Ecology. Philadelphia: W.B. Saunders Co.

Peterson, R.T. 1961. A Field Guide to Western Birds. Boston: Houghton Mifflin Co.

Robbins, C.S.; B. Bruun; H.S. Zim. 1982. A Guide to Field Identification – Birds of North America. Golden Press. New York: Golden Press.

Roosevelt, T. 1904. American Big Game in its Haunts. The Boone and Crockett Club. New York, New York.

Saunders, A. 1921. A Distributional List of the Birds of Montana. Pacific Coast Avifauna, No. 14. Berkeley, California: Cooper Ornithological Society.

Schaller, G.B. 1962. Notes on the Birds of the Southeast Arm, Yellowstone Lake. Unpublished manuscript. Yellowstone National Park Files.

Scott, S.L. 1983. Field Guide to the Birds of North America. Washington, D.C.: National Geographic Society.

Seton, E.T. 1929. Lives of Game Animals. 4 vols. Doubleday, Doran, and Co., Inc. New York, New York.

Skaar, P.D., et al. 1985. Montana Bird Distribution. Monograph

No. 3. Montana Academy of Sciences. 44. Bozeman, Montana: Montana Dept. of Fish, Wildlife, and Parks.

Skinner, M.P. 1925. The Birds of Yellowstone National Park. Roosevelt Wildlife Bulletin 3 (1). Syracuse, New York: New York State College of Forestry, Syracuse University.

Skinner, M.P. 1928. Yellowstone's Wintering Birds. Condor. 30 (July): 237-242.

Spalding, D.A. 1980. A Nature Guide to Alberta. Provincial Museum of Alberta Publ. No. 5. Edmonton, Alberta: Hurtig Publishers.

Swenson, J.E. 1975. Ecology of the Bald Eagle and Osprey in Yellowstone National Park. Master's thesis. Montana State Univ., Bozeman.

Thompson, L.S. 1985. A Harlequin Romance. Montana Outdoors Magazine (Mar.-Apr.): 21-25.

Thompson, L.S. In prep. Montana Explorers – The Pioneer Naturalists (1865-1900).

Welty, J.C. 1962. The Life of Birds. Philadelphia: W.B. Saunders Company.

Wilt, R.A. 1976. Birds of Organ Pipe Cactus National Monument. Popular Series No. 18, Southwest Parks and Monuments Association. U.S.D.I. National Park Service.

Wright, G.M. and B.H. Thompson. 1935. Fauna of the National Parks of the U.S.; Wildlife Management in the National Parks. U.S.D.I. National Park Service, Fauna Series No. 2.

YELLOWSTONE NATIONAL PARK
BIRD OBSERVATION FORM

Species:	Observer's name & Address:
Date Observed: Time:	
Specific Location in Yellowstone:	telephone number:
	Witnesses:

Describe the type of habitat where the bird was found:

Type of plumage (choose one):	Weather Conditions (choose one):
Adult Immature Juvenal	Sunny Stormy Overcast
Optics Used (choose one): Binoculars Spotting Scope Unaided Eye	If optics were used, indicate optical power:
Distance from bird:	Duration of Observation:

Number of years with previous experience with this species:

Number of times you have observed this species in the last ten years:

Describe the characteristics of the bird you observed. Record relevant information such as size, color, shape/length (bill, legs, tail), voice, behavior, number of individuals, sex, etc.

Note: All bird observations are carefully scrutinized by the Yellowstone Bird Observation Committee. YNP recommends observers and witnesses submit accurate, detailed observations and especially photographs if at all possible.

Please send this information to: Yellowstone Bird Observations
                                 Yellowstone National Park Research Div.
                                 P.O. Box 168
                                 Yellowstone National Park, WY 82190

Quick Reference
Index

Some Personal Experiences with the Birds of Yellowstone

Anyone who visits yellowstone should be aware of the unlimited number of personal observations and discoveries that add to the Yellowstone experience. Let me share with you a few of my own observations and experiences relating to the Park's magnificent birdlife.

When one counts birds, in particular species of birds, they are usually observed on a horizontal plane. This typically occurs when travelling by car or walking along a trail, but it may also occur when an observer is stationary and birds fly by a particular point (such as during migration). A rare observation I will never forget once occurred in the *vertical* plane. At noon one June day while in Mammoth I observed directly above me a pair of Common Ravens circle-soaring, but the ravens were calling repeatedly so I got out my binoculars and investigated. Above the ravens was a Red-tailed Hawk, and above the Red-tailed Hawk was a Golden Eagle, and above the Golden Eagle was a Swainson's Hawk. In less than one thousand feet above the ground I could see directly above me four species of birds in my binoculars at one time, one above the other, and all circle-soaring.

•   •   •   •   •   •   •

One day in early December a friend and I went to get a Christmas tree north of the town of Gardiner. As we drove back into the Park and through the Gardner Canyon, I noticed a Northern Pygmy-Owl perched on the top of a Douglas-fir along the Gardner River. The tree was alive but the top of the tree happened to be dead. As I mentioned to my friend, it was a "very typical place to find a pygmy-owl in the winter." I stopped the pick-up to get a better view of the little owl. I watched it for less than a minute before it flew toward us from its perch and landed on the tailgate of the pick-up, searching around the Christmas tree for prey. We watched through the back window of the truck in total astonishment, and marveled at the "false eyes" on the back of the owl's head—an optical illusion that is the owl's safeguard against predation.

That experience was the closest encounter I have ever had with a Pygmy Owl, and to this day I continually check out the Douglas-fir with the dead top, hoping to see another Northern Pygmy-Owl.

•   •   •   •   •   •   •

One of the unique features of Yellowstone is that you can travel through the same area hundreds of times and always discover something new and exciting. Such was the observation that occurred in the Pelican valley one May day. It was sunrise, and a friend and I stopped to look at a drake Blue-winged Teal in breeding plumage. We had the windows down in the car looking at the duck when we heard an incredibly loud noise resembling that of a jet. In a matter of seconds the beautiful teal was airborne and in a split second there was a phantom image of another bird that entered our view. The energetic teal could no longer be seen, but the teal's feathers were drifting in the air not far from where it took off. When the commotion settled there remained the lifeless form of a Blue-winged Teal that was being eaten by one of the most majestic birds in the world—an adult Peregrine Falcon.

Five minutes after the peregrine had begun feeding on its prey another phantom image appeared on the scene. Its entry was announced by the screeching calls of the peregrine feeding on the teal, and the introductory calls clearly identified the intruder as a Common Raven. The raven thereupon went down and stole the teal from the falcon. The peregrine in retaliation began attacking the raven by reeling in circles, continuously screaming, and diving at the raven. The raven was so alarmed by the attacking falcon that it caused the hackle feathers on its neck to rise. To avoid serious injury from the attacking peregrine the raven pulled the teal from the sandbar to the deep sedge and eventually under a willow. After ten minutes of attacking dives the peregrine gave up; the raven was lucky enough in this instance to prevail. It is difficult to believe that all of this occurred within eighty feet of our car.

●　　　　●　　　　●　　　　●　　　　●　　　　●

Observing an adult Bald eagle in flight is always a special moment. But for my wife and I an unforgettable moment of discovery occurred one August in Hayden Valley. At midday we were watching an adult Bald Eagle circle-soaring over the Yellowstone River. After about three minutes, the Bald eagle went into a spiral dive towards the water with its talons extended. It then landed in the water and grabbed a fish beneath the surface. The eagle tried to fly off but could not—the fish, which turned out to be a cutthroat trout, was too heavy for the eagle. The bird slowly floated down the river with the cutthroat in its talons, then paddled its way with its wings to a sandbar seventy feet away. The Bald Eagle dragged the eighteen-inch cutthroat out of the water and onto the sandbar. The eagle shook the water off its feathers, took off, and quickly landed on a hill. Then after feeding on the fish and reducing the weight of the prey, the bald eagle was observed circle-soaring with the cutthroat dangling from its talons.